P · O · C · K · E · T · S

CASTLES

FALCONRY

15TH-CENTURY SPANISH PLATE

14TH-CENTURY JOUSTER

WAR SWORD

P • O • C • K • E • T • S

CASTLES

Written by
PHILIP WILKINSON

LADY OF THE CASTLE

HEDINGHAM
CASTLE, ENGLAND

15TH-CENTURY "GOTHIC"
ARMOR

DK PUBLISHING, INC.

A DK PUBLISHING BOOK

www.dk.com

Project editor	Selina Wood
Designer	Janet Allis
Senior editor	Alastair Dougall
Senior art editors	Carole Oliver
	Sarah Crouch
Picture research	Victoria Walker
Production	Kate Oliver
US Editor	Irene Pavitt

First American Edition, 1997
4 6 8 10 9 7 5 3
Published in the United States by
DK Publishing, Inc., 95 Madison Avenue
New York, New York 10016

ISBN 0-7894-2047-3

Color reproduction by Colourscan, Singapore
Printed and bound in Italy by L.E.G.O.

CONTENTS

How to use this book 8

HOW TO USE THIS BOOK

These pages show you how to use *Pockets: Castles*. The book is divided into eight sections. The main sections consist of information about life in a castle and castles around the world. There is an introductory section on early castles at the front of the book and a reference section at the back, as well as a glossary and comprehensive index.

HEADING
The heading describes the overall subject of the page. This page is about castle lords. If a subject continues over several pages, the same heading applies.

CORNER CODING
The corners of the main section pages are color coded.

- ■ TYPES OF CASTLES
- ■ CASTLE DWELLERS
- ■ THE GARRISON
- ■ DAILY LIFE
- ■ ATTACK AND DEFENSE
- ■ CASTLES AROUND THE WORLD

Corner coding

Heading

Family badge

Introduction

Annotation

Military-style 'buttock' dagger

Thick, leather boots

Label

CASTLE DWELLERS

THE LORD

THE LORD spent most of his time in and around his castle. Here he would give orders to his staff who helped him look after his manor. He might also hold a local court in the castle hall, settling disputes between peasants and punishing minor crimes.

FEUDAL LORD
Even if he held only a small manor, a medieval lord was often rich and powerful. He charged his peasant tenants for services such as the use of the castle ovens, and he earned money from the estate's produce.

MANOR HOUSE
Some lords lived in a fortified manor house rather than a castle. Near the manor house was the demesne, the land reserved for the lord himself.

Caption

INTRODUCTION
The introduction provides an overview of the subject. After reading this, you should have a clear idea of what the pages are about.

CAPTIONS AND ANNOTATIONS
Each illustration has a caption. Annotations, in *italics*, point out features of an illustration and usually have leader lines.

RUNNING HEADS
These remind you which section you are in. The top of the left-hand page gives the section name, and the top of the right-hand page gives the subject heading.

FACT BOXES
Many pages have fact boxes. These provide at-a-glance information about the subject, such as how many arrows an archer usually carried.

FEATURE BOXES
These feature boxes provide additional information. This book contains a box giving details on castle loopholes.

Running head   *Fact box*

REFERENCE SECTION
The reference section pages are tinted yellow and appear at the back of the book. Here you will find useful facts, figures, and charts. These pages contain information on amazing castles, a timeline of castle warfare, and a list of useful addresses.

LABELS
For clarity, some pictures have labels. They may give extra information or identify a picture when it is not obvious from the text what it is.

INDEX
At the back of the book, there is an index. It lists alphabetically every subject included in the book. By referring to the index, information on particular topics you can find quickly and easily.

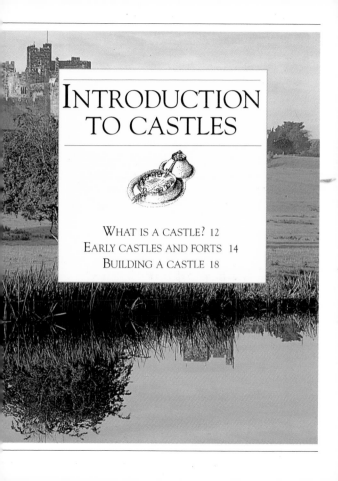

INTRODUCTION
TO CASTLES

WHAT IS A CASTLE?

A CASTLE IS A DUAL-PURPOSE BUILDING – both a fortress and a residence. Most were built during the Middle Ages (ca. 1000–1500). A castle was home to a lord and his family, and he was responsible for providing men to fight for his king. The castle was a base for these men and a local stronghold where others could shelter in times of war. Because of their two roles, castles have many interesting features that tell us a great deal about medieval life.

THE FORTRESS

A castle had to keep an enemy out and yet allow those inside to see and shoot at any attacker. The first line of defense was usually a ditch or moat, followed by a strong wall, and the last refuge was a great tower.

Siege engine

Curtain wall

Mural tower

Attackers using battering ram

Gatehouse and drawbridge

Moat

CASTLE COMPLEX

THE GREAT HALL, CHÂTEAU DE CHILLON

THE RESIDENCE

The lord's residence consisted of a hall (a combination of living room, dining room, and office) and one or more private rooms where the lord and his family slept. Nearby was a kitchen complex, which might include a pantry, buttery, brewery, and bakehouse.

LORD OF THE LAND
Castles were built in an age when warfare was conducted by mounted warriors, or knights. A castle lord, who could be any noble from a king to a lesser baron, was a knight. In addition to his military role, he managed his estate and community.

Instead of signing documents, nobles added a wax seal. This seal belonged to English knight Robert FitzWalter.

13TH-CENTURY SEAL DIE

TYPICAL CASTLE?
Castle designs vary according to the site, the fashions of the time, and the taste of the lord. This big castle would have housed a large garrison. It shows most of the features seen in this book, but many castles were less elaborate.

Chapel

Private rooms

Great tower (keep)

Great hall

Kitchen

Store-room

Prison

Garden

EARLY CASTLES AND FORTS

TRUE CASTLES were first built in Europe in the Middle Ages. But many other, much earlier structures are sometimes referred to as castles. They are usually either fortified settlements or forts built to house part of an army. They share some of the features of later castles, showing that medieval castle designers were part of a long line of fortification builders.

ORNAMENTAL STONE AT BOGAZKÖY

BOGAZKÖY, TURKEY

In the 13th century BCE, the Hittites ruled an empire based in Turkey. Their capital, at Bogazköy, was protected by stone walls with square towers. As in later castles, the fortress gates were the most strongly fortified areas.

GATEHOUSE AT BOGAZKÖY

EARLY FORT FACTS

• The stones forming Mycenae's Lion Gate, each weigh around 22 tons (20 tonnes).

• Some Roman forts covered 60 acres (24 hectares) and could house more than 5,000 men.

BUHEN, EGYPT

The ancient Egyptians built the great fortress of Buhen to defend their southern borders. It had many additions made to it during the Egyptian New Kingdom (1550–1070 BCE). The fortress was rectangular, with mud-brick walls, massive gatehouses, and square towers. Archers scanned the Nile river from the battlements.

FRONTIER FORTRESS AT BUHEN

MYCENAE, GREECE
From the 16th to the 12th centuries BCE, much of mainland Greece was dominated by small, separate kingdoms, each with its own fortified citadel. The most famous of these citadels is at Mycenae. It is surrounded by walls built of huge stones. The walls protected many houses as well as a palace.

LION GATE AT MYCENAE CITADEL

MAIDEN CASTLE, ENGLAND

Settlement   Palisade

IRON AGE FORT
During the 1st century BCE, Iron Age hill forts were built in Britain. They were protected by great earthworks (barriers made of earth) that must have taken years to construct. At the top, a wooden palisade (fence) surrounded buildings.

ROMAN FORT
The Roman legions built forts throughout Europe to a standard, rectangular plan. Some were built quickly from wood; others were more permanent structures of brick or stone.

ROMAN FORT CA. 120

More about early castles

In medieval Europe the first castles appeared in the 9th century, when the Carolingian Empire was collapsing as a result of Viking and Magyar raids. As central authority disintegrated, nobles fought for power and territory. They built castles so that they could control and defend their land. Most castles were simple, wooden structures, relying on natural defenses such as rivers or hills. Builders soon developed earthworks – mounds, banks, and ditches – for extra defense. Many castles were later rebuilt in stone, making use of the old earthworks.

Wooden tower

Motte

GERMAN MOTTE

MOTTES AND RINGWORKS
Earthworks could be mounds, called mottes, or round, raised enclosures, called ringworks. A motte housed a wooden tower; a ringwork contained buildings protected by a wooden palisade. Earth for both castle types was dug from the perimeter area, leaving a protective ditch.

STONE BUILDERS
Stone castles began to be built at the very start of the Middle Ages and soon replaced wooden castles. The earliest known stone tower was built at Doué-la-Fontaine, France, in ca. 950. Stone castles needed more workers, were more expensive, and took much longer to build than wooden ones, but were fireproof and more secure.

BUILDING A STONE TOWER

ADAPTING A MOTTE

Sometimes stone towers were built on the top of existing mottes. In the 12th century, Henry I built a shell keep (high circular wall with buildings around the inside) on William I's 11th-century motte at Windsor, England. Later, Henry II built a taller oval tower inside the shell.

Oval tower

Shell keep

WINDSOR

Motte

REUSING ROMAN FORTS

The Romans left behind many brick or stone forts, which were sometimes converted into castles in later centuries. At Portchester, England, a square Norman great tower, and other buildings, nestle in one corner of a large Roman fort.

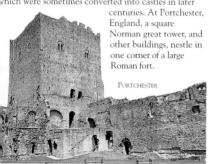

PORTCHESTER

DEFENDING A COUNTRY

Castles played a vital part in defense. An invading army had to take any castles in its path as it entered a country, a process that greatly slowed down the soldiers. If they ignored the castle, the garrisons could emerge and attack them from the rear. Otherwise, the garrisons of several castles could combine to make a formidable defensive army.

Defensive army launches counter-attack

Invading army attacks castles

BUILDING A CASTLE

THE FIRST STEP in building a castle was to choose a good site – preferably one with its own water supply and natural defenses. The lord provided the materials, but the master mason organized the workforce. Laborers hauled heavy loads from wooden scaffolding and mixed mortar. They built thick walls packed with stone rubble and flints.

MASTER MASON

CARPENTER

THE WORKERS
A small army of men was needed to build a castle. They ranged from laborers to skilled workers, such as smiths, masons, and carpenters, with a master mason in charge.

BLACKSMITH

DIVIDERS
For intricate work, a mason drew a template or plan for each stone on parchment. He then used a pair of dividers to measure each dimension on the plan and transfer the measurement to the stone.

LUMP HAMMER

Pitching tool for making clean breaks in rough stone

HAMMER AND CHISEL
Stone blocks were cut to size with a saw. The mason then trimmed them using a hammer and metal chisels. Large chisels were used for removing big chunks; smaller ones for finer work.

HAMMER-HEADED CHISELS

"Punch" for chipping off large chunks of stone

DIVIDERS

THE SQUARE
A metal square, fashioned to 90 degrees, was used to square off corners of blocks of stone.

SQUARE

SINKING SQUARE
The mason used an adjustable, or "sinking," square to measure the depth of any holes he had to cut in the stone. This tool could also be used to check right angles.

"Stock" rests on top of the stone

SINKING SQUARE

Oak stave · Wattle · Daub · Plaster

WATTLE AND DAUB
Courtyard buildings did not have to be as strong as the outer walls. Wooden frameworks were filled in with wattle (thin branches woven like basketwork) and daub (mud mixed with straw and manure), and covered with white plaster.

Blade measures depth

CONSTRUCTION SITE
In this 15th-century illustration, the lord and master mason are overseeing construction work. It could take 10 or even 20 years to complete a stone castle.

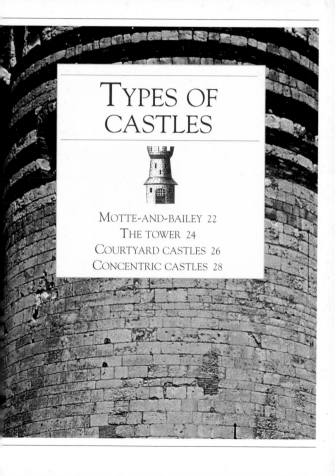

TYPES OF CASTLES

MOTTE-AND-BAILEY

MANY EARLY CASTLES consisted of an earth mound, or motte, topped with a wooden tower, and a courtyard, or bailey, which contained other buildings. Protected only by wooden fences and a ditch, these motte-and-bailey castles were vulnerable to attack by fire.

THE BAYEUX TAPESTRY

BUILDING

Motte-and-baileys could be built in a matter of weeks. When William of Normandy invaded England in 1066, he constructed Hastings and Dover Castles within two weeks of landing (above).

ANCIENT REMAINS

A ditch, motte, and earthworks around the bailey are all that remain of most motte-and-bailey castles. The flat-topped motte at Pleshey, England, is over 50 ft (15 m) tall.

Hall

Courtyard or bailey

Lifting bridge

Timber palisade

Stables

Motte

Bailey

Motte

LEWES

This unusual English castle with two mottes was built in ca. 1169 by Gulielmus de Warenne, William I's chief political officer. The mottes were made with earth from the ditches and lumps of chalk. The wooden buildings were later replaced by stone structures.

MOTTE-AND-BAILEY
The motte's tower was a refuge during war and, in some cases, housed the lord and his family. The bailey often contained a hall, buildings for livestock, a forge and armory, and a chapel.

Wooden tower on stilts

Timber walkway

MODEL OF MOTTE-AND-BAILEY

Timber flying bridge

Earth mound or motte

THE TOWER

THE FIRST STONE CASTLES were built in the 10th century and were usually centered on a large tower. The great stone tower, donjon, or keep was much stronger than its wooden predecessor, and its height gave defending soldiers a good view and better line of fire.

HEDINGHAM
Built by the Norman lord Aubrey de Vere in ca. 1140, this keep is made from a smooth stone called ashlar.

INSIDE A TOWER
A great tower provided a room for the garrison and a hall where the lord took his meals. Above the hall was the lord and lady's bedroom. From the corner turrets, guards could watch for the enemy.

Forebuilding contains entrance and extra rooms

Chapel

Curtain wall

Stair turret

Lord's sleeping accommodation

Great hall

Garrison chamber

Storeroom

Bailey

Gatehouse

A NORMAN CASTLE

ROUND TOWER
Attackers could undermine a square tower by tunneling under one corner so that it collapsed. Round towers, like this one at Pembroke, Wales, were more difficult to destroy.

PEMBROKE

TOUR DE CESAR, PROVINS

OCTAGONAL TOWER
This eight-sided tower designed by French castle builders gave defending soldiers several lines of fire.

BY THE FIRE
In a wooden hall, the fire had to be in the middle of the room, but stone towers contained fireplaces built in the wall and chimneys.

Zigzag ornamentation typical of 12th century

ROCHESTER

FIREPLACE

ROCHESTER
This huge tower, built in the 1120–30s is 125 ft (38 m) tall and has walls 12 ft (3.7 m) thick. Large windows were built on the upper floors to let in light. The windows lower down were little more then slits, to protect against enemy arrows.

COURTYARD CASTLES

SOME CASTLES CONSISTED of a courtyard protected by a strong, stone curtain wall. Along the wall were towers and usually a well-defended gatehouse. A great tower was not needed in this type of castle because a hall and other rooms were built inside the courtyard, or in the wall towers or gatehouse.

CHÂTEAU DE SAUMU

Stair tower

Well house

Defensive platform

Conical-roofed tower

Machicolations

COURTYARD WEL
At Saumur, France, a stair towe
gave access to all rooms in the
other towers and walls (above)
The well beneath the
courtyard was a vita
source of wate
during a siege

CHÂTEAU DE SAUMU
This courtyard castle
stands on a stone
platform high abov
the River Loire.
By the early
14th century,
it had large
towers with
luxurious rooms

CAERNARFON

English king Edward I built many castles in Wales during a campaign to invade and conquer the country. Some were designed as courtyard castles. At Caernarfon, the courtyard contained galleries at different heights, allowing defenders to fire from several levels.

CAERNARFON

CASTLE FACTS

• One of the gatehouses at Caernarfon contained five doors and six portcullises.
• Caernarfon cost over $3 million (in today's money) to build, but was never completed.

BODIAM

This small English castle was built in the late 14th century by Sir Edward Dalyngrygge, a local lord, as part of a plan to defend England against a possible invasion from France. The castle was defended by an artificial lake that surrounded the whole building.

CONCENTRIC CASTLES

DURING THE 13TH CENTURY, lords began to build castles with two concentric rings (one inside the other) of defensive walls. The idea may have come from knights who had seen the twin walls of the city of Constantinople (Istanbul) during the crusades.

BEAUMARIS
Concentric castles had two advantages: first, attackers had to get through two barriers; second, defending archers could stand on both sets of walls, thus unleashing more fire power. Beaumaris in Wales was built between 1295 and 1330. It had two walls, as well as a moat.

Round-shaped tower gives many lines of fire

Inner walls are almost 16 ft (5 m) thick

BEAUMARIS

Low, outer wall with mural towers

CAERPHILLY

This castle was built by English nobleman Gilbert de Clare in the late 13th century, to defend his lands against the Welsh. Concentric walls and complex waterworks make this one of the best-defended of all castles.

Low, outer wall

High, inner tower

CAERPHILLY

Leaning tower

THROUGH THE WINDOW
Windows were usually high up in the walls. Even so, they had iron bars to keep out intruders.

Arrow slits (loopholes) are narrow to protect archers behind them

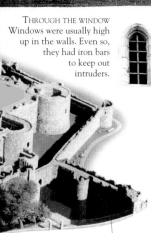

Broad moat

Barbican provides extra defense for southern gatehouse

GATEHOUSE, CAERPHILLY

GATEHOUSE
This outer gatehouse has arrow slits for defending archers and once had a drawbridge, controlled by chains that passed through holes above the doorway. Attackers had to pass through two more gatehouses in order to storm the castle.

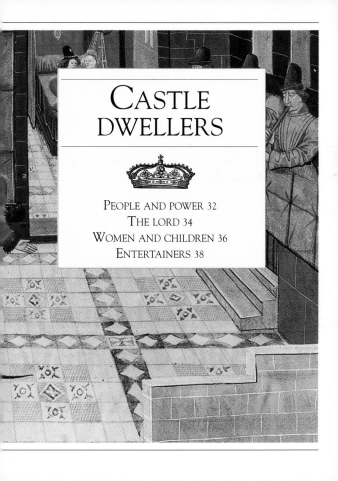

CASTLE
DWELLERS

PEOPLE AND POWER

IN THE MIDDLE AGES, land was power. All the land belonged to the king, but he gave grants of land, called fiefs, to his nobles, who built castles to defend their land. In return for land and protection, the nobles had to swear allegiance to the king and provide him with soldiers during times of war.

THE KING

BISHOPS

Bishops were as powerful as nobles and frequently acted as advisers to the king. They often lived in castles and, like other nobles, could grow rich on the taxes, or tithes, that they collected from people who lived in their area.

BISHOP

THE KING

The king was at the top of the landholding or "feudal" system. Keeping some land for himself, he built castles across his kingdom. When he visited them, his court accompanied him.

BARON

BARONS

The barons were the most powerful nobles. They held their fiefs directly from the king. In return for these large estates, each baron had to provide several thousand men to fight for the king. Otherwise, they had to pay a levy, known as a "shield money."

FEUDAL FACTS

• A noble pledged himself to be a king's servant at a special ceremony – kneeling before the king, he swore an oath of loyalty with the words, "Sire, I become your man."

• Punishments were severe for peasants who tried to leave their lord's estate.

LORD

PEASANT

LESSER LORDS

Lesser lords, or knights, held fiefs from the barons in return for military service. Unlike the barons' vast fiefs, a lord's estate could be small – often only a village, with its castle or fortified manor house.

PEASANTS

Medieval peasants were allotted small areas of land by their local lord, which they could farm. They had to give some of the produce to the lord, who owned everything they used.

THE LORD

THE LORD spent most of his time in and around his castle. Here he would give orders to his staff who helped him look after his manor. He might also hold a local court in the castle hall, settling disputes between peasants and punishing minor crimes.

Family badge

Military-style "bollock" dagger

Thick, leather boots

THE LORD

FEUDAL LORD
Even if he held only a small manor, a medieval lord was often rich and powerful. He charged his peasant tenants for services, such as the use of the castle ovens, and he earned money from the estate's produce.

SCOTNEY MANOR, KENT

MANOR HOUSE
Some lords lived in a fortified manor house rather than a castle. Near the manor house was the demesne, the land reserved for the lord himself.

3 4

THE LORD'S DUTIES

Most lords kept a close eye on the running of the estates, meeting key officials every day to check the progress of work in the fields. This French lord is discussing his demesne with one of his officials.

LORD AND BAILIFF

LORD FACTS

• If the lord was away, the constable, who was often a relative of the lord, was put in charge of the castle.

• The castle household could increase by over 100 when the lord was in residence.

OFFICIALS

The steward, one of the most important of the lord's officials, kept the accounts and organized work on the manor. The bailiff allocated jobs to the peasants, and the reeve oversaw the peasants as they worked.

Hood to keep bird calm

Felt hat

FALCONRY

Woolen, linen-lined jacket with pewter buttons

BAILIFF'S CLOTHES

RECREATION

As well as hunting with hounds, many lords enjoyed falconry – training birds of prey to catch small game. Powerful birds were very valuable; eagles were reserved for kings to fly, while ladies flew small birds such as merlins.

WOMEN AND CHILDREN

MOST MEDIEVAL WOMEN spent their lives at home, taking care of the house and children. They did everything from spinning and weaving to keeping accounts. Even so, anything a woman owned became her husband's when she married.

Jeweled headdress

THE LADY

The wife of a knight supervised the kitchens, kept the household accounts, brought up the children, and entertained guests. She also helped to run the estate when her husband was away on business or at war.

Decorated hairpins

"Horned" headdress

NOBLE FASHIONS

Most women wore woolen or linen clothes, but noblewomen dressed more fashionably. Fur-trimmed gowns and elaborate headdresses were popular in the 14th century.

Few women could read and write in the Middle Ages, but Christine de Pisan (1364–1430) made her living from writing. She wrote love poems and books on history, philosophy, and the defense of women (right).

Box hat

Woolen doublet

A boy became a page around the age of seven

Leather sandals

THE PAGE
A page was a well-born boy who was sent to live in a great lord's household to learn about life at court, including the art of courtly manners and how to serve a knight.

PLAYING THE KNIGHT
Boys of noble birth liked to play at being knights. A rich father had miniature swords and armor made for his sons; poorer boys used wooden swords.

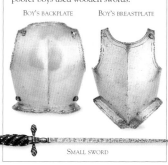

BOY'S BACKPLATE

BOY'S BREASTPLATE

SMALL SWORD

ENTERTAINERS

MINSTREL

TO WHILE AWAY the evenings, castle dwellers played games, sang songs, told stories, or listened to music provided by minstrels. Rich lords often employed their own full-time minstrels and jesters, but most were traveling entertainers, eager to "sing for their supper."

Hornpipe

THE MINSTREL
Poet-minstrels sang about love and heroic deeds, while plucking a lute or harp. Many such ballads were composed by the troubadours of 12th-century France. Musicians also played popular dances on the hornpipe (left).

ONE-MAN BAND
To accompany a dance, a musician would play a pipe with his left hand while beating a drum called a tabor with his right.

Tabor

Pipe

CHAIN DANCE
In a common 12th-century dance, the company wove in and out along a line or circle, in time to the music.

PIPES

Bagpipes were popular worldwide. The most common bagpipe had a pipe called a chanter, which was used to play the melody, and one or more drones that played a continuous note under the melody.

Drone produces single, continuous note

Bag

Mouthpiece

Chanter, used to play a range of notes

BAGPIPES

ORGANISTRUM

COURT JESTER

The job of the jester (or fool) was to make nobles laugh. He might wear bells and carry a bladder on a stick (a slapstick), and his jokes could be very crude.

COURT JESTER

ORGANISTRUM

This instrument was used in southern Europe in the 11th century. One player turned the handle, while another operated keys to play the strings.

CANTERBURY TALES

STORYTELLING

Kings or lords employed poets to tell them stories. Those who could not afford this luxury told stories to each other. Geoffrey Chaucer's *The Canterbury Tales* is a famous medieval poem about a group of pilgrims who tell each other stories to pass the time on their way to Canterbury.

THE GARRISON

MEN OF WAR

THE BODY of soldiers who lived in a castle and defended it was called the garrison. In early castles, especially in times of war, knights lived permanently in their lord's castle. Later, more knights had their own estates, and they would spend only short periods at their lord's castle.

Wheel pommel with cap

THE SWORD
The knight's main weapon was his sword, which could be wielded with one hand while he was on horseback. This double-edged weapon (left) was used to slash and cut down the enemy.

POINTED SWORD
In the 14th century pointed swords were made. They were used for stabbing between the gaps in an opponent's plate armor.

Two-handed sword

Battle-ax

FORWARD INTO BATTLE
The garrison provided a ready supply of warriors to defend the castle and lord, and to go to war. This 15th-century battle scene shows knights charging at each other with swords, battle-axes, and lances.

15TH-CENTURY FRENCH BATTLE SCENE

FIGHTING ON FOOT

The garrison included foot soldiers who fought alongside knights. They preferred staff weapons – axes, hammers, and blades mounted on poles – and a sword and buckler shield for close combat.

Single-handed sword for hand-to-hand combat

Small fist-shield, or buckler, for punching

HAND-TO-HAND WEAPONS

"BOLLOCK" DAGGER

DAGGERS

From lord to humblest soldier, most men carried a dagger. The handle was shaped to stop the hand from slipping onto the blade.

GLAIVE

This was one of the staff weapons used by medieval foot soldiers. Its pointed blade was ideal for stabbing.

GLAIVE

SOLDIERS

Most ordinary soldiers could afford only a few pieces of armor – to which they added any plates they picked up on the battlefield. A 15th-century soldier wore a quilted "jack" over his "arming" doublet, a simple helmet, and plate armor to protect his hands and arms.

"Sallet" helmet

WAR HAMMER

This hammer with sharp point could pierce plate armor. It could also concuss an opponent.

Mitten gauntlet

WAR HAMMER

Close-fitting canvas "arming" doublet

BECOMING A KNIGHT

CERTAIN NOBLE YOUTHS aged about 14 became squires, or knight's apprentices. The squire had to take care of the knight's horses and armor, and come to his master's aid in battle. He also learned warfare and horsemanship. The training was hard – not all squires succeeded in becoming knights.

DUBBING

Successful squires were knighted at around the age of 21, by another knight or the king, in a special ceremony. Before the 13th century, new knights were tapped on the head with a sword; later, on each shoulder.

TRAINING

Squires took part in sports such as wrestling, throwing javelins, stone-putting, and acrobatics. They also fought with staffs or swords. These activities kept the young men fit and helped prepare them for battle.

TRAINING FOR BATTLE

THE SQUIRE
As well as acquiring military skills, the squire had to serve his lord at the table. He was taught to be brave, protect the weak, and respect women.

ARMING A KNIGHT

One of the squire's most important duties was to help a knight put on his armor. First, the knight donned an "arming" doublet. This was a padded jacket with panels of mail under the arms and leather thongs with which to fasten armor pieces.

"Arming" doublet

CHAIN MAIL

After the leg armor was fitted, a mail skirt was put on to protect the knight's lower stomach and groin – areas not covered by plate armor.

Helmet

FULLY ARMED KNIGHT

Elbow piece attached by laces

Leather glove inside gauntlet

DRESSED FOR BATTLE

The squire helped his master put on the various sections of plate armor, which finally covered the knight from head to toe. It took a long time to put on, but was jointed to allow the knight to move quite freely.

ARMOR AND PROTECTION

THE FIRST KNIGHTS wore shirts made of mail to
protect the upper body. Soon leggings of mail
were added. In the 14th century, armor made
of solid metal plates became fashionable and
gradually replaced mail. By the 17th century,
the increasing efficiency of firearms was
making armor obsolete.

BASINET

Viewing slit

Ventilation
holes

KNIGHT'S EFFIGY
This effigy of ca. 1340 shows a
knight wearing a coat of mail
as a symbol of status.

BASINET
This typical helmet of late-
14th-century Italy gives
good protection from
arrows and sword blows.
Holes in the visor allow
the knight to see and
breathe. When the pin is
removed, the visor swings
away to one side.

Mail neck
guard

MAIL SHIRT
Mail was made up of tiny
iron rings joined together
with rivets (see below). Mail
was flexible, but heavy – a
full coat could weigh up to
31 lb (14 kg) –
and it did
not protect
against blows
from maces
and axes.

GAUNTLETS

GERMAN GAUNTLET

"Gothic-style" fluted decoration

Pointed cuff

Articulated plates

Knuckle plate

ARMORED GLOVE
This style of gauntlet, or armored glove, was popular in the 15th century. A pointed, "Gothic-style" cuff was joined to a knuckle plate by a series of articulated (movable) plates for ease of movement.

GAUNTLET PLATES
In the 14th century, knights wore thick leather gloves with metal plates attached. Plates like these covered the back of the hand; there were separate plates for the fingers. Each plate was attached to the glove with a series of metal rivets.

Brass edging

FULL SUIT OF ARMOR
In the 15th and 16th centuries, full suits of armor were fashionable. They were expensive, since a suit had to be custom-made, but they gave excellent protection from most weapons.

"Bellows" visor

Besagew to guard the armpit

Shoulder defense made from articulated plates

Cowter

Fluted decoration fashionable in 15th-century Germany

Wing on poleyn (knee guard) protects wearer from side cuts

Whole suit weighs 55 lb (25 kg)

16TH-CENTURY ARMOR

THE TOURNAMENT

Solid hammer head

TOURNAMENTS began as practice sessions for battle, but became popular courtly entertainment. Different types of combat were involved, including mock battles, jousts, and single combats; knights were sometimes killed in the fighting.

Winners often won their opponents' horses and armor.

POLEAXE
Javelins, swords, and axes were popular in foot combat. The poleaxe was used to hit an opponent on the head and could concuss a man in armor.

Blunted wooden lance

FOOT COMBAT
In foot combat with swords, each knight was allowed only a fixed number of blows. If a knight broke the rules, or if the fight got out of hand, armed guards would intervene.

RECONSTRUCTION OF AN EARLY-14TH-CENTURY JOUST

Caparison, or colorful, decorated horse covering

THE TOURNEY

In a tourney, two teams of mounted knights fought a mock battle. Many knights suffered serious injuries. Hundreds – even thousands – of knights could take part, charging at each other with lances.

TILTING HELMET

When a jousting knight charged, he lowered his head, so that he could see through his helmet's eye slit. When he raised his head, his eyes were protected by the helmet's lip.

Eye slit

FROG-MOUTHED HELMET

LANCER'S SHIELD

In some jousts, knights carried shields with curved edges to support their lances, like this one made in 15th-century Germany.

Curved edge to support lance

15TH-CENTURY SHIELD

Metal helmet

Shield painted in heraldic colors

THE JOUST

In a joust, mounted knights fought one against one. The object was to unhorse your rival with one blow of the lance. To make jousts safer, lances with blunt ends were often used.

CHIVALRY

CHAUCER'S
KNIGHT

KNIGHTS were expected to behave correctly at all times, although many knights failed to live up to this ideal. During the Middle Ages, a special code of conduct, the code of chivalry, developed. It combined military virtues with those of Christianity, calling for respect for enemies and for the weak.

CODE OF CONDUCT
The knight in Geoffrey Chaucer's *The Canterbury Tales* is courteous and merciful. He follows the courtly code conscientiously and is highly respected by his fellow pilgrims.

MYTHS AND LEGENDS
Chivalry was epitomized in heroic legends, such as the *Chansons de Geste* of medieval France and *Le Morte d'Arthur* in England. King Arthur's knights go on a quest for a lost religious relic, the Holy Grail. Only the most worthy knight, Sir Galahad, is granted a glimpse of it before he dies.

SIR GALAHAD

COURTLY LOVE
Medieval French writers developed the principles of courtly love. According to its rules, which existed more in literature than in real life, a knight vowed to be faithful to his lady.

Crusaders

Chivalric ideals influenced the founding of Christian military orders during the Crusades. These were holy wars that took place from 1095 to 1291, to take control of the "Holy Land" of Palestine from the Muslim Saracens.

CAPTURE OF JERUSALEM
The first crusaders arrived in Jerusalem in 1099. They captured and pillaged the city, founded several small states in the area, but failed to hold the city. Despite this disaster, many crusader knights stayed on in Syria and Palestine. They built castles and grew rich robbing Muslim pilgrims and traders.

Hospitaller knight

Templar knight

MILITARY ORDERS
Among the knights who settled in the Holy Land were orders of "fighting monks," who took religious vows but also fought. They included the Knights Templar, who had their base near the Temple in Jerusalem, and the Hospitallers, who specialized in healing the sick.

HERALDRY

IN THE TUMULT of a battle or tournament, it was difficul
work out who was who. So a system of symbols, called
heraldry, was devised to make the identification of
knights easier. Each noble was given a coat of arms, a
symbol that only he and his men were allowed to wear.

HERALDIC LANGUAGE
The coat of arms consisted of
a shield, a crest, and a pair of
"supporters" – figures or
animals placed on either side of
the shield. They were designed
by heralds, using colors and
patterns to represent furs, such as
ermine, and metals, such as gold.
The designs are described in a
language based on Old French.

Shield

*The symbol, or
"charge," is a
dragon, sitting
"sejant"
(erect)*

*The surface, or
"field," of the
shield is gold*

OR A DRAGON
SEJANT VERT

HERALDIC COLORS		
OR	=	GOLD
ARGENT	=	SILVER
GULES	=	RED
AZURE	=	BLUE
SABLE	=	BLACK
VERT	=	GREEN
PURPURE	=	PURPLE

AZURE A FLEUR
DE LYS (LILY) OR

ARGENT A MULLET
(STAR) AZURE

SYMBOLISM
Sometimes heralds designed visua
clues. This plate bears a shield
based on the arms of two Spanis
kingdoms. Castile is represented
by a castle and León, by a lion.
The combination of arms indicate
the marriage of two families.

BADGE OF OFFICE

Servants or men-at-arms often wore a badge bearing their lord's coat of arms. This 16th-century arm badge was worn by a servant of François de Lorraine, leader of the Knights Hospitaller in France.

Flag within a heraldic crest is quite unusual

FAMILY CREST

The crest is a symbol that was originally placed on top of a knight's helmet. It appears above the shield in a full coat of arms. This is the crest of the Churchill family. It shows a lion sejant (seated erect), with one paw raised, holding a flag.

OR A CHIEF
(HORIZONTAL SEGMENT)
INDENTED PURPURE

ERMINE (FUR) A
CROSS CROSSLET
GULES

GYRONNY
(TRIANGLES)
ARGENT AND GULES

VAIR (FUR) A
CHEVRON SABLE

Horse's heraldic covering, called a caparison

IDENTIFICATION

A knight's coat of arms could appear on his shield, or on a surcoat worn over his armor or on his horse. At a tournament, bright colors and elaborate armor were also important for identification.

THE TOURNAMENT

THE SAMURAI

THE WARRIORS of medieval Japan were called samurai. As did European knights, the samurai served a lord, rode a horse, wore armor, and lived in a castle. They wielded great power over local peasants, who grew food for the samurai.

SAMURAI KNIGHT ON HORSEBACK

MOUNTED WARRIOR
Until about 1300, the samurai fought mainly on horseback. Their principal weapons were bows and arrows, which they used against a distant enemy. Swords were used for close combat.

WAKIZASHI
A samurai warrior carried two swords sheathed in wooden scabbards. The shorter one, the *wakizashi*, was used in combat and for ritual suicide.

Sharp blade

KOZUKA

TANTO

Flecked laquered sheath

TANTO AND KOZUKA
A samurai had two knives, which he carried together in the same sheath – a dagger known as a *tanto*, and a small knife, called a *kozuka*. They had razor-sharp blades made of iron and steel.

WAKIZASHI

Wooden scabbard (saya)

EARLY ARMOR

O-YOROI ARMOR
Armor of the *O-yoroi* style was worn by samurai in the 12th and 13th centuries. It was made of small iron plates decorated with laquer.

Silk-laced sleeves

Samurai who wore this armor were mounted archers

MODERN ARMOR

The helmet has a face defense (mempo)

TOSEI GUSOKU
With the appearance of firearms during the 16th century, Japanese armorers strengthened their armor with tougher iron plates. They also introduced the *tosei gosoku* style, which included guards for the arms and legs.

KATANA
The long samurai sword was called a *katana*. The hilt was covered in sharkskin and bound with braid. This gave a rough surface that would not easily slip from the hand.

Sharkskin grip

KATANA

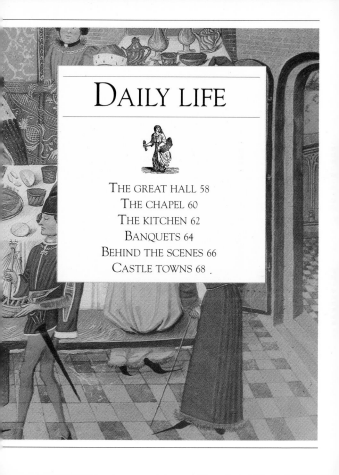

DAILY LIFE

THE GREAT HALL

THE HALL was the nerve center of the castle. Here
meals were eaten, guests were received, and castle
business was carried out; it was also used as
sleeping quarters. The castle's largest room, it
was situated on one floor of the great tower or
on its own block in the castle courtyard. It was
furnished with long trestle tables that could be
taken down at night. Around these were
benches and a chair for the lord.

ROYAL HALL
Loches Castle, France, has a 15th-
century hall used by French king
Charles VII. Its striking,
stepped roof is
flanked by round
turrets giving a
good view of the
surrounding
country.

ROYAL HALL,
CHÂTEAU DE LOCHE

BANNERS
Knights
carried
banners
into battle.
They often bore
the knight's coat of arms.
When they were not in use,
they were hung up in the
great hall for decoration.

HALL INTERIOR
The great hall at Hedingham Castle, England, takes up one floor of the great tower. Because it is on an upper floor, it has large windows. These and the big fireplace make the room seem more comfortable than most great halls.

LEGAL BUSINESS
The lord's court, held in the hall, was used for resolving local disputes. Although most lords had no legal training, they had plenty of experience of dealing with people.

FLOOR COVERINGS
Carpets were unusual in the Middle Ages. Halls on ground floors had bare floors of stone or ceramic tiles; those on upper stories had wooden floors.

FLOOR TILE

TAPESTRY AT CHÂTEAU D'ANGERS

TAPESTRIES
A hall's stone walls were sometimes decorated with tapestries. These made the room more colorful and could keep out drafts. This 14th-century example is from a series at Angers, France.

THE CHAPEL

IN THE MIDDLE AGES, everyone was expected to go to church on Sunday, so castles usually had a chapel. It could be built high in the great tower, above the gatehouse, or in its own separate building. Chapels were usually decorated with carvings, wall paintings, and sometimes stained-glass windows depicting Bible scenes.

A ciborium held consecrated bread for mass

Scene of the adoration of the Magi

Carvings of mythical beasts

MASS
Mass was held regularly by the castle chaplain. He was often the most educated resident who helped the lord write his letters.

DECORATION
Biblical scenes and mythical beasts adorn this chapel doorway at Loches Castle, France. Few people could read, so looking at carvings was an important part of education.

Henry II's knights

The assassin

Archbishop Thomas à Becket

SANCTUARY

A church or chapel was a place of sanctuary, where anyone, even a criminal, could escape the clutches of the law. In 1170, knights of Henry II of England broke the law of sanctuary, when they murdered Archbishop Thomas à Becket in Canterbury Cathedral, after he had argued with the king.

St. John's chapel

The chapel at the Tower of London is in the White Tower. Its rounded arches, cylindrical columns, and plain barrel-vaulted ceiling are typical Norman style of ca. 1090.

BURIAL

The chapel was where the lord and his family were buried when they died. Some medieval nobles were commemorated with large tombs bearing life-size sculptures of the deceased. This is the tomb of a 13th-century English knight.

COLORFUL FLOORS

Chapel walls and floors were sometimes covered with ceramic tiles. These usually bore abstract patterns, coats of arms, or Bible stories.

THE KITCHEN

IN EARLY, wooden castles, the kitchen was usually in a detached building in the courtyard, to reduce the risk of fire. In stone castles, the kitchen was often placed near the hall, separated by a narrow passage. The room contained a large fire for cooking, tables for preparing food, and ovens for baking bread. Large castles had a separate bakery and brewhouse.

KITCHEN FIREPLACE AT PFALZGRAFENSTEIN, GERMANY

BOILING
The kitchen could have several fireplaces for cooking. A small fire was used for boiling food in an iron pot. The pot was hung from a metal chain, and the heat could be adjusted by moving the hook to vary the length of the chain.

ROASTING
A popular way of cooking meat was to roast a whole carcass on a spit over a fire. Several spit-roasted animals provided enough meat for a banquet. The spit was turned by hand; it was hot, dangerous work.

Cook puts log on fire using fork

Whole carcass is roasted on the spit

COOKING A ROAST

Hollow tube removes apple core

APPLE CORER

KNIFE

FLESH HOOK

COOKING UTENSILS
In a manor or castle, head cooks were always men. They roasted, boiled, and baked vast quantities of food using large utensils such as flesh hooks. A small army of boys, called scullions, washed up.

Frame for hanging utensils

SEASONING
Herbs and spices were widely used in the Middle Ages to flavor food that could otherwise taste bland. They were also used to disguise the flavor of meat that was past its prime!

Adjustable ratchet

Small pot hanger

Large pot hook for huge cauldron

| Mint | Sage | Rosemary | Parsley |

Pot hook suspended from adjustable pot hanger

THREE-LEGGED POT
As an alternative to hanging a pot from a hook or chain, pots with legs were made to stand in the fire. Handles were added to help remove the pot from the fire.

POT HOOKS
Twin iron hooks were attached to the handles of a cauldron so that it could be hung over a fire. Several pots could be hung over a large castle fireplace.

BANQUETS

THE MAIN MEAL of the day, whether a simple dinner or an elaborate banquet, was served in the evening, in the castle hall. The grandest banquets lasted for hours.

People ate vast amounts – there were several meat and fish courses, followed by spicy or sweet puddings.

15TH-CENTURY ILLUSTRATION

SERVING AT THE TABLE
Pages and squires often served the lord and his guests at the table (left). It was common for singers and acrobats to entertain the diners between courses.

HIGH TABLE
The lord and guests sat at the high table, situated on a raised platform, or dais. The lord was the first to be served, after the food had been checked for poison by a servant taster.

Lord's seat at the center of the table

Expensive wine glass

Rabbits, coneys, were a common source of meat

LOW TABLE

Servants and other household members sat at low trestle tables set at a right angle to the high table, along the length of the hall. Food on these tables was less rich than that on the high table.

Large jug for ale

Large wooden platter

GAME

Everything from rabbits to small birds like pigeons and finches was eaten at the low table. The lord and lady were more likely to enjoy swan or fattened goose.

Pigeons were baked in hot ashes

Geese were eaten on special occasions

Spoons were placed face down to "keep the devil out"

BREAD PLATES

Food was eaten off large pieces of dry bread called trenchers. The sauce seeped into the bread, which could be eaten at the end of the course or thrown to the dogs.

Decorated ceramic jug

PLACE SETTINGS

At the high table, diners might eat off a pewter base and a wooden bowl. People used their own knives, which they carried around with them.

Wooden bowl for pottage

Drinking vessel

BEHIND THE SCENES

A MEDIEVAL CASTLE was a hive of activity. As well as men-at-arms preparing for battle, there might be builders at work, officials meeting the lord on business, and visitors from outlying estates. Many castles also echoed to the sounds of the farmyard, for animals were often kept to ensure a regular supply of food.

LONGHORN

PIG

BAGOT GOAT

CARPENTER

ANIMALS

Some animals were kept in the courtyard; others were brought in from the fields at night. Farmers made use of the whole animal, tanning the hide to make leather, and using the horns for containers.

Wool twists into yarn

SPINNING

Medieval clothes were made at home. Using a simple wooden spindle, women spun sheeps' wool into yarn, which could then be woven into cloth.

CASTLE MAINTENANCE

Damage caused during sieges or by wear and tear meant that castles had to be constantly repaired. Masons were on hand to mend stonework, and woodworkers to make doors, roofs, hoardings, and wood-framed buildings for the courtyard.

Broad ax

Private chambers

Most people slept in the place where
they worked – the cooks in the
kitchen, the armorer in his workshop,
servants in the hall. But the lord and
his family had their own rooms in a
well-defended part of the castle,
such as the great tower, the gatehouse,
or a strong wall tower.

*Urinal:
urine was
saved and
used
for cloth
finishing and
dying*

ON THE THRONE
Bathrooms were very
basic. Most castles had
garderobes – toilets
connected to a stone
chute that emptied into
a moat or cesspool.

TOOTH POWDER

CUTTLE-
FISH

WHELK

HYGIENE
Wealthy
people used
ground-up cuttlefish and
shells to make a coarse
powder for cleaning
teeth. Soap could be
made from animal
fat and wood ash.

SLEEPING ARRANGEMENTS
The lord and lady slept in
a wood-framed bed, with
woolen curtains to keep out
drafts. There might also
be a trundle bed on wheels
underneath, for children
or for servants (below).

CASTLE TOWNS

MANY MEDIEVAL TOWNS were surrounded by walls, and a castle sometimes formed part of the fortifications. It might be the home of the local lord or an official, such as a sheriff, who held the castle on behalf of the king. A sheriff kept order in the town and surrounding area. His castle was a combination of barracks, local government headquarters, residence, and prison.

CARCASSONNE
This town in southern France still has its medieval walls, with the castle adjoining them on one side. The walls and castle were built in the 12th and 13th centuries by the ruling family, the Trencavels.

Gothic cathedral

THE STOCKS

LAW AND ORDER
Criminals were often fined, but lesser crimes could be punished with a period in the stockades. The offender's ankles were locked in the manacles, and the prisoner was likely to be pelted with rotten fruit by passersby.

MARKET DAY

The right to hold a market was granted to a town by the king, in a document called a charter. A market was held once a week in the main street or central square. Traders and craftsmen set up stalls, and people came from the surrounding countryside to sell animals and produce. A market could bring great wealth to the community.

Château Comtal

PL ST JEAN R DU MOULIN D'AVER
R ST JEAN
R VIOLLET LE DUC R NOIRE DAME
R CROS MAYREVILLE R DU TRÉSAU
PL MARCOU R DU GRAND PUITS
LICES BASSES

TOWN SCENE

Gallo-Roman walls

The Great Well

Space used for crossbow practice

NIGHT WATCH

At sunset, medieval town bells rang to sound the curfew, when everyone had to be indoors. Nightwatchmen with lanterns patrolled the dark streets to deter criminals.

MEDIEVAL LANTERN

69

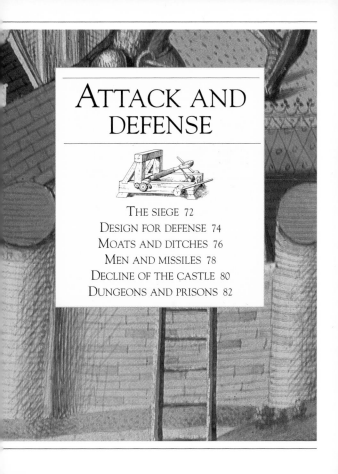

ATTACK AND DEFENSE

THE SIEGE

WHEN AN ARMY attacked a castle, it surrounded the walls so that no one could get out. Battering rams and other large weapons called siege engines were used to break into the castle. Usually, the inhabitants ran out of food and surrendered before a castle was stormed.

TREBUCHET
The trebuchet was a large wooden catapult used to hurl large stones at castle walls. It was first used in the 12th century. Several men yanked on the ropes to swing the other end of the wooden arm upward, letting loose a boulder from the sling.

Sling

Garrison defends the castle with fire

Pivoting arm

Ropes for hauling

TRACTION TREBUCHET

MINING
Under cover of a wooden shelter on wheels, attackers could dig out the foundations of a castle to make it collapse. Wooden siege towers were also wheeled next to castle walls so attackers could storm the castle.

BALLISTA

Like a giant crossbow, a ballista shot a huge metal bolt. It was not as easy to aim as a hand-held crossbow, but could be kept pointed at the gatehouse, in case the defenders tried to escape.

Rachet for keeping tension on skeins

Winch

Bow cord

BALLISTA

Rope to winch arm down

Wooden cup for missile

Skein of twisted ropes provides power

FRONT VIEW OF CATAPULT

MANGONEL

Twisted ropes provided the power for the mangonel, a type of catapult copied from the Romans. Sometimes dead animals or the heads of captured soldiers were fired over castle walls to upset the defenders.

SCALING THE WALLS

A direct, but risky, method of attack was for attackers to swarm up huge ladders. It was easy for defenders to shoot climbers or push them off their ladders.

Attackers try to storm the castle using ladders

DESIGN FOR DEFENSE

CASTLES HAD ALL SORTS OF design features to make them difficult to attack and easy to defend. Strengthened doors, openings to shoot through, holes to drop missiles or pour boiling water through – all made it hard for attackers to storm a medieval castle.

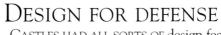

PORTCULLIS
Castles had solid doors made of wood, reinforced wth metal. There might also be one or more portcullises – grilles that could be lowered in front of or behind the door.

Slots for observation and shooting through

Wood support

WOODEN HOARDING

HOARDINGS
Wooden hoardings were overhanging structures built at the top of castle walls, to give defenders several different lines of fire. Some hoardings had holes in the floor, enabling defenders to drop stones or pour boiling water on attackers.

MURDER HOLES
Defenders might seek to trap attackers. They could then kill them by shooting arrows or pouring boiling water through ceiling holes, known as murder holes.

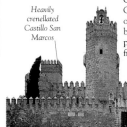

Heavily crenellated Castillo San Marcos

CRENELLATIONS
Crenellations on the top of walls allowed a soldier behind to shoot, while providing protection from enemy fire.

SPIRAL STAIRCASE
Spiral staircases in towers were built to wind clockwise. This gave a right-handed defender plenty of room to swing his sword.

MACHICOLATIONS
Many castles have machicolations – stone parapets jutting from the tops of walls. They have openings through which objects could be dropped on attackers gathered below.

FIRING MISSILES

LOOPHOLES
Narrow loopholes enabled an archer to fire, with little risk of being hit by enemy arrows. The fish-tail shape provides several angles.

EMBRASURES
An embrasure (alcove) provided room for firing. This loophole was designed for firearms.

MOATS AND DITCHES

MOST CASTLES, except those built on high hills, were surrounded by a wet moat or dry ditch. Both provided a barrier against attack, but the moat was the more effective. Moats were usually filled to a depth greater than a man's height.

WATER DEFENSES
Caerphilly Castle, Wales, is surrounded by elaborate water defenses consisting of two large lakes and several moats and ditches. A system of tunnels and sluices under the ground allowed the lord to control the water level all the way around the castle.

CAERPHILLY CASTLE

Moat is so wide it looks more like a lake

Castle is still in very good condition

CHÂTEAU DU PLESSIS BOURRÉ
This 15th-century French castle has a moat so large that many of the usual defensive features were thought unnecessary. The moat is crossed by a seven-arched stone bridge.

DRAWBRIDGE

Entry across a moat or ditch was provided by a drawbridge, which was raised to keep attackers out during a siege. The castle at Langeais, France, has twin drawbridges – a large one for horses and carts and a small one for people on foot.

MOAT FACTS

• When there was a moat as well as an earth rampart, the total height from the bottom of the moat to the top of the rampart was at least 30 ft (9 m).

• Moats were sometimes drained and filled in by attackers during a siege.

Gardens planted in the courtyard

CHÂTEAU D'ANGERS

Semicircular mural tower

Bridge, site of original drawbridge

Broad, dry ditch

DITCHES

The castle at Angers, France, is surrounded by a broad ditch. Ditches were often given sheer stone sides and lined with pointed wooden poles to slow the enemy down.

MEN AND MISSILES

WHEN A CASTLE was attacked, the enemy was usually at a distance, so crossbows and longbows were fired from loopholes around the outer walls. The garrison might also go out on sorties (sudden attacks), picking off as many of the enemy as they could before retreating back inside the castle gates.

WINDLASS
A crossbow was so powerful that some form of machine was needed to pull the cord back ready for firing. A common method of doing this was to use a windlass. This device (left) has handles that the archer turns.

Windlass cord

WINDLASS

CROSSBOW
The crossbow fired metal bolts. It was a powerful, deadly weapon but took time and effort to reload after firing. This was a handicap on the battlefield but did not matter in a castle because the archer could hide behind the walls while reloading.

Stirrup

Three spikes rest on the ground

Arrows could fly 984 ft (300 m)

Barbed arrow-head

CALTROPS
Made of iron, caltrops were designed so that one spike pointed upward when it was thrown on the ground. Defenders scattered them outside the castle gate when an attack was expected. They could badly injure men and horses.

German halberd ca. 1500

HALBERD
This weapon was used by foot soldiers. Its steel blade could inflict nasty injuries on both men and horses. The halberd could also be used to pull a knight from his horse.

LONGBOW
The longbow was a favorite weapon of English armies from the 14th century onward. It was light and fast but required strength from the archer.

LONGBOW

ALL-PURPOSE

THIN BODKIN

Fragment of shaft

BROADHEAD

ALL-PURPOSE

BODKIN

ARROWHEADS
Made of iron, fine-pointed arrowheads came in various shapes. Broadheads could severely injure horses; bodkins could get through mail; thin bodkins could pierce plate armor.

ARCHER FACTS
• Up to 12 arrows could be shot from a longbow in the time it took to load and shoot a single crossbow bolt.

• An archer usually carried 12 arrows, but might shoot others he found on the battlefield.

DECLINE OF THE CASTLE

EUROPEAN SOCIETY became more peaceful during the late 15th century. As a result, nobles looked for more comfortable homes. War was increasingly fought by professional soldiers based in forts, so castles became less important. Some were turned into luxurious palaces. Others fell into disrepair, and their stones were used to construct new buildings.

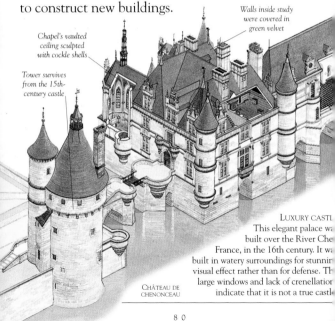

Walls inside study were covered in green velvet

Chapel's vaulted ceiling sculpted with cockle shells

Tower survives from the 15th-century castle

CHÂTEAU DE CHENONCEAU

LUXURY CASTLE
This elegant palace was built over the River Cher, France, in the 16th century. It was built in watery surroundings for stunning visual effect rather than for defense. The large windows and lack of crenellation indicate that it is not a true castle.

Grande Galerie added by Catherine de Medici

THE DAWN OF FIREARMS

Firearms were first used in Europe in the 14th century. Large ones like cannons could damage castle walls, but did not make castles obsolete – soldiers were still better protected behind stone walls than out in the open.

HANDGUNS

Early handguns were used to attack and defend castles. Inside a castle, marksmen fired through special keyhole-shaped loopholes. Later, guns were used in batteries (groups) for which forts were specially designed.

Iron barrel

Deal Castle's low, curved walls deflected cannon balls

Heraldic badge to identify the marksman's lord

RISE OF THE FORT

In the 16th and 17th centuries, forts such as Deal Castle, England, were built for batteries of guns. They were built (by the state) at strategic points, purely for defensive purposes, not as residences.

DEAL CASTLE

81

DUNGEONS AND PRISONS

SINCE CASTLES WERE secure buildings, they could be used as prisons. This did not happen often, as criminals in the Middle Ages were usually punished by fine or execution. But sometimes political prisoners were held in a castle, or criminals kept there before a trial. Most castles did not have custom-built dungeons, so prisoners might be held in any secure room.

TORTURE CHAMBER
Torture was unusual in medieval castles, but in later years, the rack was used to force prisoners to reveal military secrets or renounce religious beliefs.

DUNGEON FACTS
• Some dungeons were called *oubliettes*, a French word meaning "locked away and forgotten."
• Many underground vaulted passages thought to be dungeons are actually drains.

IN CHAINS
Very dangerous criminals were not only locked in a cell – they were also restrained by leg irons or a heavy iron collar and chain.

Locking iron collar weighed 35 lb (16 kg)

Heavy iron chain attached to wall

HELD FOR RANSOM

Nobles captured in battle were held in a castle until ransom money was paid for their return. They were usually kept in good conditions – a dead prisoner brought no ransom. The Duke of Orléans was held in the Tower of London after the Battle of Agincourt (1415).

Heavy grille made of hardwood

Wooden peg

Window

BARRED VIEW

In the prison at Loches Castle, France, one cell is entered through a barred door made of solid strips of oak. Inside the cell, a stone bench is the only furniture, and light enters through a small, barred window.

THE DUKE OF ORLÉANS HELD FOR RANSOM

Part of castle containing prison

THE PRISON

At Loches, a strong tower next to the keep was used as a prison and torture chamber from the 15th century onward. The paintings of one 16th-century prisoner, the Duke of Milan, can be seen on the walls of his dark cell.

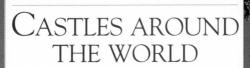

CASTLES AROUND THE WORLD

BRITAIN AND IRELAND

WHEN THE NORMANS invaded England in 1066, they built castles all over the country. Many of their great towers still survive, often surrounded by later curtain walls. Castle building continued throughout the Middle Ages, with a boom during the 13th century, especially in the reign of Edward I (1272–1307), who developed castle design in Wales.

Mound contains remains of original motte-and-bailey

14th-century gatehouse had portcullises and murder holes

Guy's (sandstone) Tower contained rooms for the garrison

Armor

Great Hall, rebuilt in the 1800s

WARWIC
The first cast
on this site was
motte-and-bailey built
William I in 1068. In the 12th centu
stone walls were added, with further towers
sandstone appearing in the 14th century. The ea
wall, with its massive gatehouse, dates from this peric

Low curtain walls, good for firing from, but not for defense

CASTELL-Y-BERE

CASTELL-Y-BERE
This castle was built by the Welsh lord Llwelyn the Great in the 13th century. It has a large, D-shaped tower, typical of Welsh castles. The castle's construction follows the shape of the rock on which it was built.

HARLECH
Edward I ordered Harlech Castle to be built in 1283. His master mason, James of St. George, created a strong, concentric design with strong towers and an enormous gatehouse. The castle withstood several lengthy sieges.

HARLECH'S GATEHOUSE

COLCHESTER
Britain's largest Norman great tower was built at Colchester, on the foundations of a disused Roman temple. The tower was originally about 90 ft (27.5 m) high, but the top two stories were pulled down in 1683.

TOWER OF LONDON
This famous royal castle, one of the best-defended in Britain, was begun by the Normans. They built the great tower, called the White Tower, while the surrounding concentric walls were added during the reign of Henry III (1216–72).

TOWER OF LONDON

Scotland

Stone castles were rare in Scotland until the 13th century, but the Scots quickly learned from English and French designs. By the time Edward I of England invaded Scotland in 1296, he had to attack many castles. During the 14th century, the Scottish tower house emerged.

Crenellated parapet for sentries

TRAQUAIR
Many tower houses, such as that at Traquair, were extended to provide more living space. At Traquair, the windows were also enlarged and the battlements demolished to provide extra room in the attic.

NEIDPATH
Tower houses were buil to deter local attacks rathe than major assaults. The hal and other living rooms wer built one above the othe with crenellations and arrow loops toward the top (above)

EDINBURGH
Once the residence of Scottish kings, this castle was begun in th 6th century on an outcrop of roc overlooking the city. The preser buildings date from the 12th to 20th centuries.

EDINBURGH

Ireland

For centuries, the Irish defended themselves with earthworks and wooden ramparts, which often surrounded an entire town. Motte-and-bailey castles were also widely built, hundreds of years after they had fallen out of favor in the rest of Europe. However, many stone castles were also built in Ireland, by English and Norman rulers.

KILKENNY
With its drum towers and tall walls, this castle retains much of its medieval form. The large windows were added much later.

CARRICKFERGUS
Built in the late 12th century by the Anglo-Norman leader John de Coucy, this large castle defends the entrance to Belfast Lough. It has a Norman great tower and a later twin-towered gatehouse.

Great tower

Kitchen

Stables

Bakery

Gatehouse built ca. 1250

Chapel

CARRICKFERGUS

FRANCE

THE COUNTRY that gave Europe feudalism, France is home to some of the earliest castles. Rivalry between the powerful counts of Anjou and Blois led to the building of many castles in the Loire region. The trend continued when England fought France in the Hundred Years' War (1337–1453).

CHÂTEAU D'AZAY-LE-RIDEAU
In the 16th century, French lords built castles with large windows and comfortable staterooms. At Azay-le-Rideau, built between 1518 and 1527, defensive features were merely decorative.

CHÂTEAU DE CHINON
The vast structure overlooking the Vienne River is actually three castles. Two were built by the counts of Blois; one, by the counts of Anjou. In the 12th century, Henry II ruled both France and England from Chinon.

CHÂTEAU DE CHINON

CHÂTEAU DE GOULAINE

CHÂTEAU DE GOULAINE
Goulaine was originally built in the 14th century, but buildings date from the 14th to 17th centuries. It withstood a famous siege during the Hundred Years' War, in which the lady of the castle, Yolande de Goulaine, threatened to kill herself if the defenders did not fight the English.

CHÂTEAU DE LOCHES

CHÂTEAU DE LUYNES
The 13th-century castle walls and towers of this castle, built by the first Duke of Luynes, still survive, although they now have large windows. Originally, there would have been crenellations beneath the conical roofs.

CHÂTEAU DE LUYNES

TOWN OF LOCHES
The ancient 12th-century tower of Loches Castle is typical of early French square keeps. It is surrounded by later curtain walls and mural towers built by French monarch Philip Augustus. These walls were extended around the medieval town.

CHÂTEAU D'AINAY-LE-VIEIL
This eight-sided courtyard castle retains its 13th-century outer walls, with their arrow slits, crenellations, and massive towers. The gatehouse, guarded by a drawbridge, is also original.

CHÂTEAU D'AINAY-LE-VIEIL

VIANDEN

SCANDINAVIA AND THE LOW COUNTRIES

FEUDALISM CAME LATER to these lands than to the rest of Europe. Castles in Belgium and the Netherlands were the work of feudal lords, while in Scandinavia, kings and church leaders were the main castle builders. Most of these castles are in low-lying regions so many have water defenses. Because of a lack of good building stone in Belgium and the Netherlands, castles tended to be built of brick.

VIANDEN, LUXEMBOURG
One of Europe's smallest countries, Luxembourg, contains one of its largest castles, Vianden. Built in the 11th century, it has a hall that seated 500 and a chapel with a trapdoor leading to an underground vault.

MUIDERSLOT

MUIDERSLOT, NETHERLANDS
This rectangular Dutch courtyard castle is surrounded by a moat. Like many castles in the region, it is built of brick. This well-preserved structure dates from the late 14th century although there has been a castle on the site for around 1,000 years

KALMAR, SWEDEN

This was one of several castles built to protect the Swedish coast from pirates in the 12th century. Artillery bastions were added in the 16th century. The castle has withstood 20 sieges.

KALMAR

EGESKOV

BEERSEL, BELGIUM

Belgium's Beersel Castle was captured twice during a revolt in 1489, at which time it suffered considerable damage. Most of the current castle, with its corner towers, stepped Flemish gables, and broad moat, dates from the rebuild of 1491. The large towers were designed to provide plenty of accommodations.

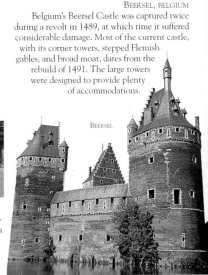

BEERSEL

EGESKOV, DENMARK

Built in 1554, this is one of the best-preserved lake castles. It is built on a foundation of oak piles, rammed down into the mud at the bottom of the lake. Its walls contain secret staircases and embrasures.

GERMANY

MEDIEVAL GERMANY was divided into dozens of tiny independent states, many of which had their own castle. In the 11th century, lords began to build a typically German type of castle with a slender tower, or *Bergfried*, often built on a hilltop. The shape of the castle was thus governed by the site; symmetrically planned castles were rare until the late Middle Ages.

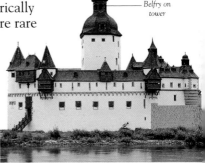

HEIDELBERG
This castle was home to the Counts Palatine of the Rhine valley, who ruled this area in the Middle Ages. Built on a rocky outcrop, it overlooks their capital, the city of Heidelberg. They extended the castle during the Renaissance period.

Belfry on tower

GERMAN CASTLE FACTS

• The German states were under the general rule of the Holy Roman Emperor; both the emperors and individual rulers built castles.

• The Hohenstaufen family built castles across Germany and Italy (from 1152–1250).

PFALZGRAFENSTEIN
King Ludwig I of Bavaria built this castle in the middle of the Rhine in 1327. Pflazgrafenstein was originally intended as a base for officials collecting tolls from ships on the river.

BURG ELTZ

When a German noble family grew, several brothers could inherit a castle and divide it among them. This type of castle was called a *Ganerbenburg*. Burg Eltz was occupied by six branches of its ruling family, each of which had a house in the courtyard.

Bergfried

LICHTENSTEIN

BURG ELTZ

LICHTENSTEIN

Three branches of the same family lived in this castle, resulting in an irregular mixture of buildings clustered around its *Bergfried*. Access was by way of a wooden bridge.

MARKSBURG

The Marksburg is typical of many German castles that grew gradually over the centuries. It was begun in the 13th century, when the tall tower was built on a high crag above the Rhine. The courtyard was added in the 14th century.

MARKSBURG

CENTRAL AND EASTERN EUROPE

LIKE GERMANY, MUCH OF THIS AREA was part of the Holy Roman Empire during the Middle Ages, and natural features such as hilltops and crags were used to enhance fortifications. In low-lying areas, water defenses were popular, and many castles were built near lakes.

CHILLON

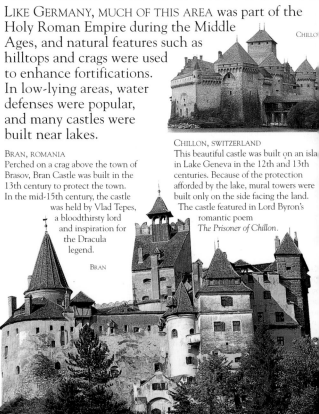

CHILLON, SWITZERLAND
This beautiful castle was built on an isla in Lake Geneva in the 12th and 13th centuries. Because of the protection afforded by the lake, mural towers were built only on the side facing the land. The castle featured in Lord Byron's romantic poem *The Prisoner of Chillon*.

BRAN, ROMANIA
Perched on a crag above the town of Brasov, Bran Castle was built in the 13th century to protect the town. In the mid-15th century, the castle was held by Vlad Tepes, a bloodthirsty lord and inspiration for the Dracula legend.

BRAN

MARIENBURG, POLAND

This is one of several castles built by the religious military order the Teutonic Knights in the 14th century. It has several typical features, being a brick-built courtyard type with a large chapel.

MARIENBURG

DÜRNSTEIN

DÜRNSTEIN, AUSTRIA

Richard I of England was held prisoner at Dürnstein on his return from the Third Crusade. The castle had two walls, one at the bottom of the cliff on which it stands, the other halfway up. Some of the walls were destroyed by mining in the 13th century.

KARLSTEJN, CZECH REPUBLIC

Originally built in the 14th century by Charles of Hungary, this castle near Prague combines strength and elegance. Built on a craggy hill, its massive keep was protected by five large towers and high curtain walls.

SPAIN

FOR MUCH OF THE MIDDLE AGES, Christians fought the Moors (Muslims) for control of Spain. Both sides built castles and copied each other's ideas on fortification. The Moors liked to build square or wedge-shaped enclosures. The Christians introduced the great tower, or *torre del homenaje* (tower of homage).

Torre del homenaje *usually had pointed roofs*

ALCÁZAR OF SEGOVIA
In the 11th century, the Christians took Segovia from the Moors and built this stronghold. It is in the form of a *gran buque* (great ship) castle a long building, tapering toward one end.

Pointed crenellations

CASTILLO DE COCA
This castle is built of brick – even the moat has a brick lining. It was constructed for Alfonso de Fonseca, Christian archbishop of Seville, but has many examples of Moorish motifs.

CALATRAVA LA NUEVA
Spain's military order, the Knights of Calatrava, built this huge castle as its headquarters in 1217. It reveals a mixture of European and Moorish styles.

ALHAMBRA
The Alhambra was built by the Moorish rulers of Granada in the 15th century. It has luxurious halls and courtyards, and beautiful fountains.

Hall of the Ambassadors

Hall of the Two Sisters

Hall of the Abencerrajes

Court of the Lions

Council chamber

Court of the Myrtles

26 round towers give defenders excellent lines of fire

PEÑAFIEL
This 15th-century castle is a *gran buque* design. It is a massive structure, 690 ft (210 m) long. The castle has a 111 ft- (34 m-) high great tower, and 26 round towers.

ITALY

IN THE MIDDLE AGES, Italy was made up of small independent states, often based around fortified towns. As time went by, lords strengthened the walls of their town homes, creating Italy's first true castles. Some had a great tower with curtain walls. Others were courtyard castles with heavy wall towers. Holy Roman Emperor Frederick II built many castles in Italy during the 13th century.

CASTEL SANT'ANGELO, ROME
Raised on the site of Roman buildings, this great fortress was extended throughout the Middle Ages. Once home to the city's chief noble family, it was later taken over by the popes, who lived there during times of unrest.

Hall of Columns had good views over the whole city

Luxurious halls added by 15th- and 16th-century popes

CASTEL SANT'ANGELO

SAN GIMIGNANO TOWERS

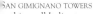

In this small Italian town, rival families built a total of 72 towers, 14 of which are still standing.

Rival lords showed off by building towers taller and taller

Octagonal satellite tower *Octagonal courtyard*

CASTEL DEL MONTE

Frederick II chose an unusual octagonal design for Castel del Monte in southern Italy. The castle, begun in 1240, is fortified with thick walls and eight turrets for archers. The rooms inside were once very luxurious.

FLOOR PLAN

The plan of Castel del Monte shows eight vaulted rooms, one on each octagonal face.

CASTEL NUOVO, NAPLES

Remodeled by Alfonso I of Aragon, who used both Spanish and Italian builders, this castle has a triumphal arch, built to commemorate Alfonso's entry into Naples in 1443.

CASTEL NUOVO

THE MIDDLE EAST

CRUSADERS WERE IMPRESSED by the huge Byzantine and Muslim fortifications they encountered on their expeditions, and took over these strongholds to encourage European settlers. They built castles to guard roads and to help them attack nearby towns. By the late 12th century, such castles were being used as border posts, administrative centers, and army bases.

QATRANA, JORDA
Qatrana is a typical Musli
fortress. Its plain, rectangul
walls were difficult to attac
The castle was protecte
with arrow slits, pointe
crenellations along th
tops of the wall, ar
machicolations abov
the doorwa

VAN, TURKEY
Many Middle Eastern castles were used by different peoples as the area passed from one ruling power to another. Van Castle in Turkey was first built during the Byzantine period, in 850. In the Middle Ages, the Seljuk Turks took it over and extended it, and they were followed by the Ottoman Turks. Armenian Christians later lived in the castle.

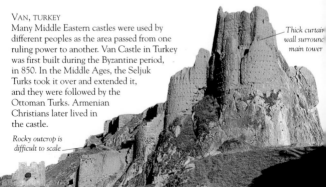

*Thick curtain
wall surround
main tower*

*Rocky outcrop is
difficult to scale*

Square, main tower

CRUSADER CASTLES

- More than 40 crusader castles were built along the coastal strip of the eastern Mediterranean.

- Many castles had huge storerooms: the defenders of Baghras Castle, Turkey, stowed away 12,000 sacks of grain in case of siege.

KERAK, JORDAN

Built by crusaders in 1142, Kerak is located near routes used by Muslim traders and pilgrims. Its garrison, led by their lord, Reynald de Chatillon, frequently raided passersby. This infuriated the Muslims, who laid siege to Kerak in 1183 and 1184. The final siege in 1188 lasted for eight months and led to the fall of the castle.

Medieval core of castle

Courtyard

Wall walk

Round bastion added by Venetians

KYRENIA, CYPRUS

Crusaders built this castle on the northern coast of Cyprus in the late 12th century. It had a stormy history, finally being modernized by a garrison from the rich trading city of Venice in the 16th century.

Krak des Chevaliers

Krak des Chevaliers (Castle of the Knights), in Syria, was built by the Knights Hospitaller. The knights lived like monks but took up arms in defense of crusaders or Christian pilgrims. Thought by T. E. Lawrence (Lawrence of Arabia) to be "the best preserved and most admirable castle in the world," Krak withstood Saracen attacks until 1271. It fell only because the garrison was tricked into surrender by the sultan Beibars.

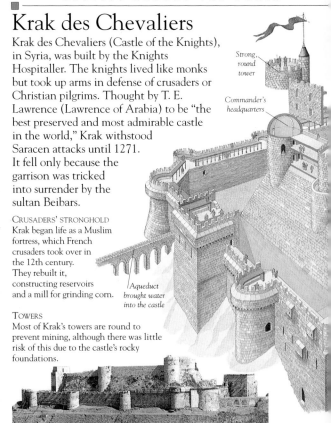

Strong, round tower

Commander's headquarters

Aqueduct brought water into the castle

CRUSADERS' STRONGHOLD
Krak began life as a Muslim fortress, which French crusaders took over in the 12th century. They rebuilt it, constructing reservoirs and a mill for grinding corn.

TOWERS
Most of Krak's towers are round to prevent mining, although there was little risk of this due to the castle's rocky foundations.

Main hall was used for meals and meetings

A strict religious order, the Hospitallers had a large chapel

PLAN
A plan of the castle shows two lines of concentric walls, with a narrow entrance that was easy to defend. The hall, chapel, and commander's room are in the heart of the castle.

Wall towers gave good vantage points

Dark passage

Batter (slope) makes walls difficult to scale

ENTRANCE
The castle entrance is overlooked by battlements and arrow slits. Even if an enemy got past these, he was faced with a walk along a narrow, covered passageway that bent back on itself. This was kept dark so that attackers would be almost blinded as they emerged into the light of the courtyard.

Arrow slits were placed all around walls

JAPAN

IN THE 16TH AND 17TH CENTURIES, a political system developed in Japan that was very similar to European feudalism. Local lords built large castles to provide security during periods of political unrest. These castles had tall wooden towers with overhanging roofs. The towers were set in stone-walled courtyards that often had many inner walls and side towers so that enemies could be trapped there and kept away from the main tower.

MATSUMOTO

HIMEJI

Outer courtyard is intended to trap enemy

MATSUMOTO

This 16th-century castle has a vast wooden tower and side towers. Galleries run around each floor, protected by wooden shutters. The lord favored archers, because their weapons were silent, so the walls have narrow slits.

Nijo

Castles like Nijo, which dates from 1603, were built using a framework of strong wooden beams. The dimensions were carefully worked out, giving Japanese castles an elegance often lacking in their European counterparts. The luxurious interior of Nijo is decorated with landscape paintings.

Nijo

Himeji

One of Japan's largest castles, Himeji began as a small fortress in the Middle Ages, but was extended in the 16th and early 17th centuries by warlord Ikeda Terumasa. The central, wooden tower contains rooms for the lord, his family, and samurai warriors. The walls are covered in plaster to reduce the risk of fire.

Elaborately decorated roof indicates that lord is of high rank

Side corridors provided well-protected firing platforms

Side tower gives a good view of enemy approaching from the east

Hidden doors under the roof could be lifted up to give a clear view of the enemy below

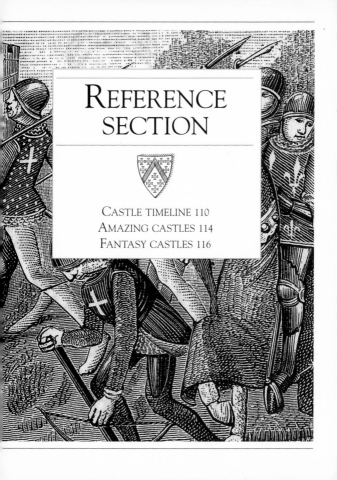

REFERENCE SECTION

CASTLE TIMELINE

THIS TIMELINE traces the development of castles
and castle warfare. Castle design changed greatly,
from simple wooden tower with enclosure and ditch,
to massive stone tower surrounded by walls and moat.
Castles were later superseded by the palace and fort.

476–864	911–1037

476–864

• 476 End of the Roman Empire.

• ca. 700 Introduction of stirrups to
Europe from Asia helps horsemen fight
from the saddle.

• ca. 800 The emperors of
the Carolingian Empire
defend their realm from
Viking and Magyar
invasions with mounted
cavalrymen – the first
knights. Feudalism develops in Europe.

CAROLINGIAN
KNIGHT

• ca. 800–1150 The Romanesque style
of architecture is fashionable in Europe.
Typical Romanesque features appearing
on castles include semicircular arches,
round-headed windows, and barrel
vaults. In England, the Romanesque
style is often called "Norman."

• 864 Charles the Bald, ruler of the
western part of the Carolingian
Empire, orders that castles built
without his consent be destroyed.

911–1037

• 911 Rollo, Viking chieftain, settles in
northwestern France; his followers
become the first Normans.

• ca. 950 Earliest known stone tower is
built at Doué-la-Fontaine, France.

• 987–1040 Foulques Nerra, Count of
Anjou, builds 27 castles as part of his
campaign against the Count of Blois.

• ca. 1000 The Normans start to build
castles in many parts of Europe; they
favor motte-and-bailey designs and
strong, stone great towers.

• 1000–1200 Italian towns,
such as Florence,
Rome, and Venice,
become independent
city-states.

MOTTE-AND-BAILEY

• 1037 Fernando of Castile conquers
the kingdom of León, northern Spain,
greatly extending Christian power in
the area.

1066 –1113	1118–1180

• 1066 William of Normandy invades England and builds castles all over the country.

• 1095 The crusading movement begins; Europeans build castles in the Holy Land. They also bring back Eastern ideas about fortification to Europe.

• ca. 1100 Tower keeps become increasingly common in much of Europe. Archers become important in warfare.

STONE TOWER

• 1100 German lords begin to build tall, slender towers (*Bergfrieder*), often sited on high, craggy hills for natural defense.

BATTERING RAM

• 1100–1200 Simple siege engines, such as battering rams and siege towers, are used to attack castles.

• 1113 The Knights of St. John, or Knights Hospitaller, are founded in Jerusalem. They protect Christian pilgrims and fight on behalf of crusader kingdoms in the eastern Mediterranean. They build some of the most notable castles in the area.

• 1118 The Knights Templar are founded to protect Christian pilgrims in Palestine. Their name comes from the fact that their first house was built on the site of the Temple in Jerusalem.

• 1140s European crusaders build several castles in the eastern Mediterranean; the most common design is a rectangle with a tower at each corner.

• 1142 Crusaders take over Krak des Chevaliers in Syria.

KRAK DES CHEVALIERS

• 1150–1500 The Gothic style of architecture becomes fashionable in Europe. This style is typified by pointed arches and ribbed vaults.

• 1160 Henry II of England experiments with new tower designs, including the many-sided keep at Orford, Suffolk.

• 1169 First Norman invasion of Ireland finds the Irish relying on walled towns and wooden fortifications.

• 1180–1226 Reign of Philip Augustus of France, who builds many castles.

1190–1270	1270–1337

1190–1270

• 1190 The Teutonic Order of Knights is founded in Germany to defend Christian lands in Syria and Palestine. They build many castles, especially in eastern Europe.

• 1190s Courtyard castles increase in popularity as the focus of defense shifts away from the great tower and toward stronger walls and gatehouses.

• 1196–8 Richard I builds Château Gaillard in France; the castle, one of the strongest to date, pioneered the use of inner and outer defenses that were designed to work together.

• 1200s Rounded wall towers begin to be built, and brick castles appear in the Netherlands.

TOWER AT PEMBROKE

• 1220–1250 Reign of the Holy Roman Emperor Frederick II, who builds numerous castles in Germany and Italy, and experiments with new designs.

• 1266 Siege of Kenilworth Castle, England, lasts six months – one of the longest sieges on record.

• 1270s Machicolations begin to replace wooden hoardings.

1270–1337

• 1270–1350 Concentric plans become fashionable, and curtain walls of many castles are strengthened.

• 1271 Krak des Chevaliers falls to the Muslims (Saracens).

• 1272–1307 Reign of Edward I of England, who is well known for his castle building in Wales.

• 1291 End of the Crusades.

BEAUMARIS CASTLE

• 1300s Emergence of the Scottish tower-house.

• 1304 More sophisticated siege machines, such as catapults, become widespread.

• 1320s Cannons first used in Europe.

• 1330 Plate armor in widespread use.

14TH-CENTURY GAUNTLET

• 1337–1453 The Hundred Years' War between France and England stimulates castle building and developments in warfare.

1347–1453	1476–1900

• 1347–51 The Black Death kills 25 million people across Europe.

GUNLOOP

• 1380s Gunloops first built into castles, as at Carisbrooke, Isle of Wight, England.

• 1400s Castle building is in decline in Europe.

• 1415 At the Battle of Agincourt, English longbowmen triumph over the French. Mounted knights begin to decline in importance on the battlefield.

• 1418 The English besiege Château Gaillard, France, for 16 months; the garrison finally surrenders due to lack of water.

LONGBOW ARCHER

• 1450 Many castles walls are made thicker to cope with the destructive power of artillery.

• 1453 Ottoman Turks capture the city of Constantinople (modern Istanbul), bringing the Byzantine Empire to an end.

HAND GUNNER

• 1476–7 In the wars between France and Burgundy, pikemen and hand gunners win many victories over knights.

• 1492 Spain's Christian rulers, Ferdinand and Isabella, conquer Granada, the last bastion of the Moors. This completes the Christian reconquest of Spain.

• 1500s Comfortable palaces take precedence over castles across Europe.

• 1509–1547 Reign of Henry VIII of England, who builds forts (such as Deal and Walmer castles) to defend England from possible invasion; no one lives in these buildings, which are essentially firing platforms.

HIMEJI

• ca. 1600 Great age of castle building in Japan.

• 1600s French military genius Sebastian le Pestre de Vauban designs star-shaped forts.

• 1800s Renewed interest in castles as symbols of the medieval world. Ludwig II, the "mad" king of Bavaria, builds his "fairy-tale" castles in Germany.

AMAZING CASTLES

SINCE MEDIEVAL TIMES, castles have witnessed countless thrilling events – sieges, executions, ghostly visitations – and many strange tales are told concerning them. Here are a few of the most intriguing.

WORLD'S LARGEST CASTLE

The largest ancient castle in the world is Hradcany Castle, in Prague, Czech Republic. It was originally constructed in the 9th century, and has retained churches, chapels, halls, and towers from every period of its history. The castle covers about 20 acres (8 hectares).

HRADCANY CASTLE

LEFT TO ROT

During the 13th century, Templar Knights were imprisoned in Chinon Castle, in France. They were left to starve, and the castle walls still bear the writings of the knights facing their doom.

DEATH BY RED-HOT POKER

Berkeley Castle, England, is famous for the ghastly murder of Edward II by order of his wife. While he was sleeping, a red-hot poker was forced into his bowels.

THE GRAY LADY OF GLAMIS

Glamis Castle, Scotland, is said to be one of the world's most haunted castles. Among its ghosts are the cruel "Earl Beardie," a tongueless woman, a lady in white, and the Gray Lady, thought to be Lady Glamis who was burned alive as a witch in Edinburgh over 400 years ago.

LOVE TRIANGLE

Two ghosts are reported to haunt the magnificent Château de Chenonceau, France. Catherine de Medici, wife of Henry II, reappears under a full moon, combing the hair of her rival, Diane de Poitiers, the king's beautiful mistress. When Henry died, his jealous wife exiled Diane from the château, the one place she truly loved. Diane's sad ghost is seen, at the time of the full moon, standing before the mirror in her bedroom.

DIANE'S GHOST

DREAM CASTLE

Neuschwanstein Castle in Germany was one of several fantastic castles created by King Ludwig II of Bavaria, who ruled his country, reluctantly, from 1864 to 1886. Inspired by Wagner's operas, the castle was designed by a Munich scene painter and built to look like a medieval castle, although it was a lot more luxurious inside. Walt Disney's famous castle logo was inspired by this castle.

NEUSCHWANSTEIN

MAGICAL KISS

It is said that whoever kisses the magical stone at Blarney Castle, Ireland, will acquire magical eloquence. The stone is set in the wall below the castle battlements. In order to kiss it, a visitor is grasped by the feet and suspended backward under the parapet.

TALL STORY?

According to legend, when Richard I of England was imprisoned in Dürnstein Castle, Austria, for over a year, his minstrel, Blondel, searched for him everywhere. He sat outside castle walls and sang Richard's favorite songs. Eventually, he heard the king join in, and realized that he had found his lord.

GREAT ESCAPES

Colditz Castle, Germany, stands on a great rock overlooking the Mulde River. Dating back to 1028, it has many secret passages that were used in sieges. During World War II, it was a high-security prisoner camp. Though the castle was allegedly escape proof, a number of Allied prisoners managed to get out.

PRINCES IN THE TOWER

English king Richard III was said to have ordered the murder of his nephews, Edward V and Richard, in the Tower of London in 1483. The princes were kept there to prevent nobles from trying to put Edward on the throne. Who really killed them, and when, is a mystery.

TOWER OF TERROR

The Tower of London was a royal residence, armory, treasury, and prison for enemies of the crown. Many were brought by boat from trial at Westminster Hall to the infamous entrance, Traitors' Gate. Notorious traitors were executed on nearby Tower Hill, and their heads displayed on poles as a grim warning to others who might challenge the sovereign.

HEADS ON POLES

FANTASY CASTLES

CASTLES PROVIDE spectacular settings for many romantic legends and swashbuckling tales. In fairy tales, castles are often enchanted places where dwell demons, orgres, or captive princesses. Some novelists portray them as sinister places fraught with terrors.

CAMELOT

CAMELOT
King Arthur's magical castle and court was known as Camelot. From here the noble knights of the Round Table rode forth to find the Holy Grail. Various British locations have been suggested as the possible site of this mythical castle. They include Caerleon Castle in Wales, Tintagel in Cornwall, and Cadbury Hill in Somerset.

SCOTT'S ROMANTIC NOVELS
The Scottish novelist Sir Walter Scott wrote about the lives of castle dwellers in his swashbuckling novels, *Ivanhoe* (1820), *Kenilworth* (1821), and *Castle Dangerous* (1831). Based on historical events, the books feature some real-life figures as characters.

EPIC POEMS
During the Middle Ages, poets wrote long, narrative poems that glorified chivalric behavior. The French *Song of Roland* and the Spanish *Poem of the Cid* are both about knights in the time of feudalism. They tell of the storming of castles and wars against the Moors.

SHAKESPEARE'S CASTLE DRAMAS
Much of the action in Shakespeare's plays takes place in castles. The murder of King Duncan in *Macbeth* (ca. 1608) occurs at Glamis Castle, Scotland. *Hamlet* (ca. 1608) is set at Kronborg castle in Denmark, known as Elsinore in the play. Hamlet first sees the terrifying ghost of his murdered father, the king of Denmark, while walking on the castle battlements. The ghost urges Hamlet to avenge the foul crime by killing the murderer – Claudius, Hamlet's own uncle.

HAMLET

CHÂTEAU D'USSÉ

SLEEPING BEAUTY

Built in 1462 as a castle and later ornamented with turrets, towers, and windows, the Château d'Ussé inspired Charles Perrault to write *The Sleeping Beauty*. It overlooks the River Indre in western France. Other fairy tales, such as *Puss in Boots*, and *Beauty and the Beast* feature enchanted castles with strange or sinister occupants.

GOTHIC CASTLE STORIES

Regarded as the first Gothic novel, Horace Walpole's *Castle of Otranto* (1764) is set in 12th-century Italy. It pits the villain Manfred against an innocent heroine, Isabella. In film adaptations of Mary Shelley's novel *Frankenstein* (1818), the setting for the scientist's monstrous experiments is a remote castle. In *The Pit and the Pendulum* (1843), by Edgar Allen Poe, a prisoner of the Spanish Inquisition is held at Toledo Castle. He awaits death by a razor-sharp swinging pendulum in a rat-infested dungeon.

FORBIDDEN ROOMS

A castle's secret rooms and nooks and crannies make it a mysterious place. In the Finnish fairy tale *The Heart's Door*, a young man is given the keys to 24 extraordinary rooms in a copper castle. He is told that he can enter the 24th room "at his own risk." Curiosity gets the better of him, and he unlocks the door. Inside he finds a lovely woman, but the path of true love is not smooth.

BLUEBEARD

In the French story *Bluebeard*, the contents of a secret chamber are not as agreeable. Bluebeard's new wife is forbidden access to "the little room." When she peers inside, she sees the bodies of her husband's former wives. The same fate now beckons her.

DRACULA

DRACULA'S CASTLE

One of the classic horror stories, Bram Stoker's *Dracula* (1897), would not be the same without its sinister castle setting. The story was inspired by the cruelties of the sadistic Transylvanian prince Vlad Tepes or "Vlad the Impaler" (1430–76). Based at Bran Castle, he reigned for less than ten years, yet his insatiable lust for blood may have caused at least 50,000 deaths.

Resources

Tourist information centers throughout Europe can give you information about castles. Museums are another useful source.

ORGANIZATIONS

English Heritage
Customer Services
429 Oxford Street
London, W1R 2HD
English Heritage is responsible for many English castles. As well as providing information, it operates a membership program, with free admission to properties.

Friends of Historic Scotland
Room 214
20 Brandon Street
Edinburgh, EH3 5RA
Many castles are in the care of Historic Scotland.

Cadw: Welsh Historic Monuments
Brunel House,
2 Fitzalan Road
Cardiff, CF2 1UF
Many Welsh castles are in the care of Cadw.

National Trust
36 Queen Anne's Gate
London, SW1H 9AS
The trust owns several castles in England.

MUSEUMS

British Museum
Great Russell Street
London, WC1B 3DG
Britain's national museum provides historical background information on the Middle Ages.

Metropolitan Museum of Art
1000 Fifth Avenue
New York, New York 10028
Arms and armor collection – with examples from Europe, the Middle East, and Asia – is one of the most encyclopedic in the world. Medieval art is housed in both the main building and the Cloisters, which incorporates 2 chapels and elements of 5 cloisters into its structure.

Museum of London
London Wall
London, EC2 5HN
Modern museum covering the history of the capital: includes much information about the medieval period relevant to the history of the castle.

Royal Armouries
Armouries Drive
Leeds
West Yorkshire, LS10 1LT
Houses one of the finest collections of arms and armor in the world.

CASTLES TO VISIT

BRITAIN
Tower of London
London
Famous royal castle with Norman White Tower. Houses the Crown Jewels, ravens, and other exhibits

Dover Castle
Dover
Huge castle with large tower and later curtain walls; hosts events in which medieval warfare,

jousting, and scenes from daily life are reenacted.

Warwick Castle
Warwick
Magnificent fortress with state rooms, armory, and wax figures to illustrate its history.

IRELAND
Blarney Castle
Blarney
Famous for the Blarney Stone, which visitors can kiss. Little remains of the castle except the keep.

FRANCE
Château de Loches
Loches
Medieval town with magnificent castle boasting the deepest dungeons in the Loire.

Château de Saumur
Saumur
Celebrated fairy-tale château with guided tour.

Château de Chenonceau
Chenonceau
Lavish château and gardens

stretching across the River Cher.

ITALY
Castel del Monte
Località Andria, Bari
One of the most sophisticated secular buildings of the European Middle Ages.

Castel Sant'Angelo
Rome
From dank cells to fine apartments of Renaissance popes, the castle museum covers all aspects of the site's history.

GERMANY
Neuschwanstein
Füssen
Famous fairy-tale castle in the Bavarian mountains. Luxurious rooms are open to the public.

Burg Eltz
Münstermaifeld
Spectacular castle set in woods. Guided tours show original furnishings, wall hangings, and paintings.

SPAIN
Alhambra
Granada
A magical use of space, light, water, and decoration characterizes this sumptuous palace.

Alcázar of Segovia
Segovia
Spectacular castle built on rocky outcrop, with typical Spanish design features.

CZECH REPUBLIC
Hradcany
Prague
Still housing a presidential office, this huge castle has galleries and museums.

ROMANIA
Bran
Bran
A superb medieval castle and home of the Dracula legend.

SWEDEN
Kalmar
Kalmar
This magnificent 13th-century coastal castle has survived 20 sieges.

Glossary

ARTILLERY
Firearms, such as handguns and cannons.

ASHLAR
Building stone precisely cut and finished to a smooth surface.

BAILEY
Castle courtyard usually associated with a motte.

BAILIFF
Person in charge of allotting work to peasants, organizing repairs to castles, and doing other jobs on a medieval estate.

BALLISTA
Siege engine taking the form of a giant crossbow.

BARBICAN
Outlying defense, usually in the form of a walled courtyard protecting a castle gate.

BARREL VAULT
Tunnel-like (barrel-shaped), semicircular stone ceiling.

BARTIZAN
Corner turret projecting from a high wall, popular in Spanish castles.

BASINET
Close-fitting medieval soldier's helmet, with a visor.

BASTION
Tower projecting from castle wall.

BATTERING RAM
Large beam used to break down the walls or doors of a fortification.

BATTLEMENT
Parapet on top of a castle wall, with a series of gaps, allowing defenders to shoot through; alternative term for crenellation.

BERGFRIED
Type of German castle with a slender tower.

BREWHOUSE
Building or room where ale was brewed.

BUTTERY
Chamber used for storing and preparing food and drink.

CAROLINGIAN EMPIRE
Dynasty that ruled in France and Germany from 751–987.

CHÂTEAU
French word for castle; now often used to describe a country or manor house.

CHIVALRY
Medieval principles of knighthood.

CITADEL
Stronghold within, or close to, a city.

CONCENTRIC CASTLE
Castle with two or more concentric (with the same center) walls.

CONSTABLE
Official put in charge of a castle while his lord was away. Also known as a castellan.

COURTYARD
Walled enclosure containing a great hall and other buildings.

COURTYARD CASTLE
Type of castle consisting of a courtyard and a stone curtain wall.

CRENELLATION
Battlements on top of a castle wall.

CROSSBOW
Weapon with a bow arranged at a right angle to a wooden stock; it was used to fire metal bolts.

CURTAIN WALL
Outer wall of a castle.

DESMENE
Area of land reserved for a lord.

DIVIDERS
Instrument with two pointed arms, used for measuring or dividing lines.

DONJON
Another name for great tower or keep.

DRAWBRIDGE
Lifting bridge that can be raised to keep out an enemy.

DRUM TOWER
Semicircular or rounded tower.

DUBBING
Ceremony in which a monarch or high-ranking lord gives another person the title of knight; usually involves tapping a new knight on each shoulder with a sword.

EARTHWORK
Fortification made of earth mounds, banks, and ditches.

EMBRASURE
Alcove in inner wall where archers can load their weapons and fire.

ENCLOSURE
Castle courtyard.

FALCONRY
The practice of keeping falcons and training them to hunt. Now a sport, in medieval times, falconry was used as a way of hunting.

FEUDALISM
Social system operating in the Middle Ages, according to which land was granted to nobles in return for services.

FOREBUILDING
Structure or building protruding from the front of a great tower, containing the entrance and, often, the chapel.

FORT
Fortification designed to protect defenders who did not usually live there.

GANERBENBURG
German castle divided into several dwelling units, each occupied by a different branch of a family.

GARDEROBE
Lavatory.

GARRISON
The soldiers who manned and occupied a castle.

GATEHOUSE
The entrance building in a curtain wall; usually one of the most heavily fortified parts of a castle.

GAUNTLET
Armored glove, often with long cuff.

GRAN BUQUE
Type of Spanish castle in the shape of a ship.

GREAT TOWER
Main tower of a castle, often containing a hall, a lord's private chambers, storerooms; also known as a keep.

HALL
Main reception room of a castle, used for meals, meetings, and formal occasions. It also served as a sleeping area for servants.

HERALDRY
The system of coats of arms used to identify noble families.

HOARDING
Timber structure projecting from the top of a wall, used as a firing platform.

JOUST
Combat, put on for entertainment, in which two knights rode toward each other with lances.

KEEP
Alternative name for great tower.

KNIGHT
Man who served his lord as a mounted warrior.

LONGBOW
Large, powerful wooden bow, used to shoot arrows, often over long distances.

LOOPHOLE
Narrow opening through which defenders could shoot.

LORD
Any male member of the nobility or knighthood, often holder of a castle or manor.

MACHILOCATION
Projecting stone structure on top of wall from which defenders could drop missiles on those below.

MAIL
(OR CHAIN MAIL)
Flexible armor made of interlocking metal rings.

MANACLE
Lockable metal ring used to secure the hands of a prisoner.

MANGONEL
Siege engine in the form of a stone-throwing catapult.

MASON
Skilled stoneworker.

MILITARY ORDER
Organized group of fighting monks, who took religious vows but also participated in certain types of warfare.

MINING
Tunneling under a castle wall in order to weaken the foundations and bring the castle down.

MOORS
The Muslim ruling class of Spain during the Middle Ages.

MOTTE
Natural or man-made mound on which a castle was built.

MOTTE-AND-BAILEY
Wooden castle based on an earth mound and an adjoining courtyard.

MURAL TOWER
Tower projecting from the curtain wall of a castle.

MURDER HOLE
Opening in ceiling through which defenders could fire or drop missiles on enemies below.

OUBLIETTE
Dungeon, often reached by a trapdoor in a floor.

PAGE
Young boy of noble birth who served in the household of a lord, and sometimes became a squire.

PALISADE
Strong wooden fence.

PARAPET
The wall protecting the outer side of a wall walk.

PEWTER
Metal alloy, often containing tin, lead, and copper.

PIKEMAN
Soldier carrying a pike or similar long-handled weapon.

PLATE ARMOR
Armor made of jointed metal plates.

PORTCULLIS
Grille that could be lowered at a castle gate to keep out enemies or trap them in a gatehouse.

POTTAGE
Thick soup.

RAMPARTS
Earth banks surrounding a castle.

REEVE
Peasant appointed as supervisor of work on the lord's land.

RIBBED VAULT
Stone ceiling with a supporting network of protruding stone structures called ribs.

RINGWORK
Round castle consisting of a circular rampart and wooden fence, protecting a slightly raised courtyard.

SAMURAI
Japanese mounted warrior.

SHELL KEEP
Round stone structure containing lean-to buildings, erected on a castle motte.

SHERIFF
Royal official, based in a castle, who was in charge of law and order.

SIEGE ENGINE
Large weapon or device, such as a battering ram or big catapult, used to attack a castle.

SIEGE TOWER
Wooden tower on wheels that attackers used to climb over castle walls.

SMITH
Person who worked with metal.

SQUIRE
Young man who served a knight, helping him with his horses and armor, who hoped to become a knight himself.

STEWARD
Official in charge of the running of a lord's estate; managing work, keeping accounts, etc.

TORRE DEL HOMENJA
Spanish term for great tower or keep.

TOURNAMENT
Event featuring jousts and mock battles held for entertainment and as practice for warfare.

TOURNEY
Mock battle staged as part of a tournament.

TOWER HOUSE
Form of small castle, common in Scotland, consisting mainly or entirely of a single tower.

TROUBADOUR
Poet-musician of the Middle Ages, especially one who specialized in songs of courtly love.

TURRET
Small tower sticking out from a wall, often containing a staircase.

VAULT
Arched structure that forms ceiling.

VISOR
Flap on a helmet that can be pulled down to protect the face.

WALL WALK
Path along the top of a castle wall.

WINDLASS
Winding mechanism, such as that used to load a crossbow.

Index

Acknowledgments

Dorling Kindersley would like to thank:
Hilary Bird for the index; Château de Saumur, Cotswold Farm Park, Gordon Models, Château de Loches, Museum of St John, Order of The Black Prince, Pitt Rivers Museum; Caroline Potts for picture library services; Tanya Tween for design assistance and special photography by Jerry Young. Robert Graham and Natasha Billing for research.

Illustrations by:
Janet Allis, David Ashby, Stephen Biesty, Joanna Cameron, Brian Craker, John Crawford-Fraser, Paolo Danati, Brian Delf, Peter Dennis, Will Giles/Sandra Pond, Chris Orr, Kevin Robinson, Nick Shewring, Mike Taylor, Eric Thomas.

Photographs by:
Max Alexander, Peter Anderson, Geoff Brightling, Joe Cornish, Geoff Dann, Mike Dunning, Steve Gorton, Paul Harris, John Heseltine, Alan Hills, Paul Kenward, Dave King, Neil Lukas, Liz Macaulay, Steven Oliver, John Parker, Martin Plomer, Rob Reichenfeld, Dave Rudkin, Tim Ridley, Kim Sayer, Micheal J. Waterman.

Picture credits:
T=top b=bottom c=center l=left r=right
Hunting Aerofilms Ltd: 23tc, 23cl. AKG London: 59tr. The Ancient Art and Architecture Collection Ltd: 12cl, 15tr, 55tl, 60tl, 61br, 68bl, 96tr, 97cl, 102b, 107tl. The Bridgeman Art Library: British Library/Bridgeman Art Library London: 16br building Marseilles, 32br Archbishop of Arundel, 33br June mowing, 35tl Le Rustican du Cultivement des Terres, 37tr Christine De Pisan, 39br Lydgate and the Canterbury pilgrims, 40–41,

42br 15th-century battle, 50cr lady and her lover, 56–57 tapestry Dukes of York, 62bc roasting spit. 64tl Richard III, 72cr siege tower. Bridgeman Art Library, London: 50tl Canterbury Tales. 70–71 capture of Acre. Biblioteca Estense, Modena/Bridgeman Art Library: 45br Sungod. Bibliotheque Nationale Paris/Bridgeman Art Library: 19br tapestry of stone masons. 51tr Pillage of Jerusalem. Hedingham Castle/Bridgeman Art Library, London: 59tl Great hall. Lauros Girandon/Bridgeman Art Library: 30–31 tapestry, 59br River of Paradise. V & A Museum/Bridgeman Art Library, London: 32cl, Henry VI at Westminster. ©British Museum: 13tc, 61tl. The Danish Tourist Board: Lennard 93cl. ET Archive: 73br. The J. Allan Cash Photolibrary: 17bl, 93br, 96bc, 97br. JNTO: Bill Hobdell 84/85, 106cl. © Museum of London: 63tl. Loches Castle : 82r. By courtesy of Luxembourg National Tourist Office: 92tl. Michael Holford: 22tr, 34br, 61bl. National Guild of Stone Masons: 18bl, 18bfl, 18br, 18bfr, 19tl, 19cl. Robert Harding Picture Library: 83cl, 94tr. Board of Trustees of the Armouries: front cover cr, 55r, 55bl, 79bc. Sonia Halliday Photographs: 103b, 103tl, 104bl. Crown Copyright/ Historic Royal Places: 61tr. Wales Tourist Board: 25tr. Reproduced by permission of the Trustees of the Wallace Collection: front cover cl, 2tr, 2br, 37br, 37bc, 42cl, 42c, 46c, 46/47b, 47r, 47tl, 48tl, 49cr, 49c, 52bl, 79cl. Weald & Downland Open Air Museum: back cover tc, 19cr 64/65b, 65tr, 67tl, 67br. York Archaeological Trust 63br, 65br. Zefa Pictures: 101tl, 82tl, 92bl, 93tc, 95tl, 95tr, 97tc.